Deadly Transfers and
the Global Playground

Deadly Transfers and the Global Playground

Transnational Security Threats in a Disorderly World

Robert Mandel

 PRAEGER

Westport, Connecticut
London

Library of Congress Cataloging-in-Publication Data

Mandel, Robert, date.
  Deadly transfers and the global playground : transnational
security threats in a disorderly world / Robert Mandel.
      p.   cm.
  Includes bibliographical references and index.
  ISBN 0–275–96228–8 (alk. paper)
    1. National security—International cooperation.   2. Security,
International.   3. Subversive activities.   4. Crisis management.
  I. Title.
  UA10.5.M325   1999
  327.1'7—dc21   98–46794

British Library Cataloguing in Publication Data is available.

Library of Congress Catalog Card Number: 98–46794
ISBN: 0–275–96228–8

First published in 1999

Praeger Publishers, 88 Post Road West, Westport, CT 06881
An imprint of Greenwood Publishing Group, Inc.

Printed in the United States of America

The paper used in this book complies with the
Permanent Paper Standard issued by the National
Information Standards Organization (Z39.48–1984).

10 9 8 7 6 5 4 3 2 1

Contents

Figures

Preface

As has been the case with my previous four books, this volume results from both (1) considerable dissatisfaction with dominant trends in the literature on international conflict and security issues and (2) considerable passion to try to help security policy makers grapple with a complex and confusing set of emerging threats. Academic scholars generally seem to have difficulty quickly fine-tuning their conceptual lenses to cope with a rapidly changing global setting, and government officials frequently find themselves needing to contain and forestall dangers without the analytical tools they need to place individual incidents in a broader perspective. This problematic predicament provided a persistent prodding for pursuing this project.

During the last half-decade I have published several pieces which helped to shape the thinking that emerges here: *The Changing Face of National Security* (Greenwood Press, 1994), "What Are We Protecting?" (*Armed Forces & Society*, 1996), "Perceived Security Threat and the Global Refugee Crisis" (*Armed Forces & Society*, 1997), "Exploding Myths About Global Arms Transfers" (*Journal of Conflict Studies*, 1998), and "Deadly Transfers, National Hypocrisy, and Global Chaos" (*Armed Forces & Society*, 1999). In the process I have had conversations with numerous colleagues both here and abroad in government and university settings who have significantly contributed to my thinking, and I wish to thank them collectively for their help. However, I take full responsibility for any egregious errors found here. There is no question in my mind that the thinking presented in this volume will need further refinement.

Introduction

There seems to be a continued disconnect between the current predicament in the global security environment and both theoretical and case-specific writings in the field. Among the theoretical pieces, which constitute a tiny minority of what emerges here, much of the literature is still state-centric (assuming that we can largely direct our attention to the behavior of nation-states) or oriented toward the emergence of international security regimes that have somehow never quite made their appearance on cue. Among case-specific pieces, many exhibit an ostrich-like tendency to treat illuminating analysis on one narrow piece of the complex post–Cold War security puzzle in complete isolation, not interconnecting it with other related pieces so that the broader pattern becomes evident. As a result, policy makers attempting to cope in a practical way with ongoing security challenges often do not find the kind of relevant overarching insight that they desperately need.

Since the end of the Cold War, an important shift has occurred in the global setting that demands a fresh, holistic analysis. Relationships among nations have often failed to follow expected patterns, and non-nation-state actors have proliferated and become more influential. The resulting reduction in the dominating role of national governments has left somewhat of a vacuum of global authority and power, with no one (including the United States, most frequently called upon to assume the role of world policeman) willing to step in to fill the void. In opposition to the growth of international interdependence and the emergence of regional blocs integrating states together from the outside, we witness the growth of subnational separatist movements fragmenting states from the inside. The net effect of this setting is anarchy, tension, and conflict.

Recently, cross-national transactions have risen dramatically in conjunction with the growth of global interdependence. Within these flows across boundaries are many that are not under national governments' exclusive initiation or control. While many of these transnational flows seem quite beneficial, some appear dangerous because they violate national laws and global norms; create potentially devastating political-military, economic, social, or environmental effects; and are virtually impossible to monitor and prevent. This set of pernicious transfers has largely escaped scholarly scrutiny because of their elusive surreptitious nature.

This study provides an integrated explanatory analysis of the new global security environment, which it terms "the global playground," and the consequent blossoming of these flows, which it terms "deadly transfers." The analysis is explicitly theoretical rather than historical, attempting to detect and evaluate broad overarching patterns in this crucial context. It begins by discussing the general nature of the emerging global playground and the deadly transfers that occur within it, and then turns to an overarching analysis of the intractable causes, pernicious consequences, and futile cures associated with these ominous transnational flows. Next, it presents brief overviews of the most important flows—clandestine conventional arms, illegal human migrants, illicit psychoactive drugs, unsanctioned hazardous materials, lethal infectious diseases, and incapacitating information disruptions. It then highlights the national hypocrisy associated with the deadly transfers and the crippled international rules of the game associated with the global playground. Throughout this analysis the threats to the security protection goals of biological survival, political authority, and socioeconomic cohesion play an important role. Finally, the study concludes by analyzing the security implications of this predicament, with (1) a discussion of the challenges involved in converting the global playground and its deadly transfers into a civil community characterized by mutually uplifting beneficial transactions and (2) a set of prescriptive ideas about how to augment our conventional ways of responding to this kind of threat.

The brief examination included of the six flows' special features facilitates consideration of their broader relationship to the coherence of national and international security policy. Because of the covert nature of these transactions, the details are inherently speculative and largely anecdotal. However, the discussion of the general trends, illustrative examples, and distinctive security issues involved in each type of transnational transfer conveys at least a general sense of their interwoven threat.

This study is distinctive in a number of ways. By using the image of the playground, it attempts to communicate just how far from the ideal of authoritative order the global setting has strayed and just how misguided are our images of safety in the international environment. In highlighting the threat of deadly transfers, it tries to indicate how pervasive and deep has been the abandonment of the ideal that transactions must restrict themselves to sanctioned activities, and how truly dangerous this deviation has been for the proper functioning of all aspects of civil society. In addressing national hypocrisy and crippled global rules of the game related to these activities in this setting, it does not shy away from pointing directly at potential areas of security dysfunction at all policy-making levels. In analyzing all of the major ominous transnational flows, it endeavors to knit together the idiosyncratic patterns associated with each one to uncover common parallel tendencies associated with all of them and to explore the tight linkages among them. In taking a largely theoretical rather than case-specific approach to exploring these issues (admittedly there is no real choice available here because the absence of reliable data eliminates the possibility of a thorough and comprehensive empirical analysis), this study hopes to escape from the usual purely descriptive laundry list of shocking anecdotal incidents to develop a broader and more probing understanding of the new security dilemmas confronting us all.

Finally, in highlighting the futility of existing remedies to the deadly transfers and suggesting an alternative preliminary and tentative set of ideas to cope with these transactions, this study tries to widen the arsenal of security policy makers in the ways they have available for responding to these ominous transnational flows. In particular, the originality of the set of responses introduced lies in their movement away from traditional top-down increases in inhibitions related to elite-dominated system structure and in their movement toward bottom-up decreases in instigations related to mass-oriented individual attitudes.

In many ways this study is highly tentative because it is only recently that attention has focused on the issue, and both existing theory and existing evidence on the topic are sketchy. This volume sets up propositions analyzing the dynamics of deadly transfers on the global playground that are subject to both criticism and revision. In the end, the hope here is to stimulate both curiosity and dread about an intriguing transactional facet of the world in which we live.

Deadly Transfers and the Global Playground

Chapter 1

The Emerging Global Playground

For many of us, contemplating playground imagery conjures up a flood of positive nostalgic memories. When we think of our past experiences on playgrounds at schools and city parks, fond, wistful memories surge forward about happy carousing with friends during recess, bright sunny days filled with playing ball and screams of delight, and a totally carefree and secure enjoyment of leisure time. If these euphoric reminiscences were accurate in characterizing the current situation, then there would be no mention of the playground environment in this book.

Unfortunately, the reality of playgrounds in both school and park settings today has changed dramatically. Violence and physical fighting abound, often with knives and guns readily available, so much so that stabbings and shootings that occur there in major cities no longer make the headlines. Playgrounds are often favorite spots for gang activities, especially involving the sale of drugs, and in school settings unauthorized parties often enter the premises unnoticed. Taunting, bullying, and mean-spirited transmission of false rumors about others is commonplace, and the noise and commotion prevent effective communication from one part of the playground to another. If any disease is present, it spreads like wildfire on the playground, given the close and uncontrolled activities that take place. Frequently people will use playgrounds as dumping grounds for garbage and other hazardous materials because they want to save the money associated with proper disposal or because they simply do not care about the effects on others.

Playground monitors, who used to provide a guarantee of order in case something went wrong, are virtually nonexistent in park playgrounds and at schools are sparse and distracted; given what goes on, many of these monitors have learned to stand together talking to each other, seemingly intentionally not noticing all the problems that are transpiring. Such behavior might not be as irresponsible as it initially appears; for monitors to intervene in some of the dangerous activities on the playground might very well place them in immediate peril. Moreover, the problems that exist here are so deep-rooted that in many ways it would seem foolhardy to believe that the solution lies in dramatically increasing the number of monitors present.

The spirit of anarchy prevails, and nobody in his or her right mind would go to a playground after dark. Indeed, many students at schools stay in their classrooms rather than face the threatening environment present during recess, and many parents will not let their children play on public park playgrounds at any time during the day. Because society in general seems to harbor a glorified view of the virtues of playground activities, does not really have any direct knowledge of what goes on in playgrounds, or views playgrounds as unworthy of scrutiny because they are simply places where free-choice leisure time activities take place, it has largely ignored the severe problems that exist here.

THE RELEVANCE OF THE PLAYGROUND METAPHOR

This study contends that the playground is an appropriate metaphor to characterize the current global security setting in which deadly transfers flow in ever-increasing quantities from place to place. Despite the recent paucity of formal international wars, civil strife and ethnic violence have escalated significantly since the end of the Cold War, fueled by growing clandestine shipments of conventional arms to the regions of turmoil. Terrorist

groups spread political disruption and transnational criminal organizations spread economic disruption on a scale unprecedented
in recent decades. Rogue states and deviant individuals wreak
more diversified havoc in the international arena. Illegal migrants
sneak in record numbers across national borders. The flow of illicit
narcotics across national boundaries has reached an all-time high.
Information disruptions are on the rise, as disruptive forces take
pleasure in interfering with the tightly interconnected electronic
communication system upon which the functioning of modern society increasingly relies. With the huge increase in global travel,
epidemics of infectious diseases have become all too familiar. As
places to dump hazardous materials vanish, unsanctioned transfers overseas increase, endangering the survival of both people
and the natural ecosystems in those places unlucky enough to
become the final destination points.

As with school and park playgrounds, there are many in the
world within both governments and the general public who are
in denial about this current predicament, preferring to take a blind
eye to these dangerous emerging trends and to sustain a more
optimistic view of the global system. The dominant view among
members of this hopeful group is one laced with pride about the
inexorable progress of human civilization over time. This school
of thought would forcefully argue that the manner in which this
study uses the playground metaphor is overdrawn and overly
pessimistic. The supporting assumptions of this position include
the spread around the world of the norms and values present in
advanced industrial societies, the growth of integrated international interdependence, and—perhaps most importantly—the
global endorsement (at least rhetorically) of the seemingly stabilizing principles of democracy and capitalism. The group of analysts focusing on the role of international organization appears to
be particularly susceptible to this rosy image that the global community is marching headlong toward greater enlightenment, buttressed by their view that the United Nations is growing in
strength, a new world order is emerging, characterized by collective security arrangements, and informal transnational regimes are
developing on cue to manage problems that span national borders. From this self-satisfied perch, anarchy is becoming extinct.
When confronted with evidence about the deadly transfers, those
buying into this positive perspective calmly respond that these

types of transactions have occurred throughout human history and that humanity is now in a better position than ever to nip what they characterize as small atavistic irregularities in the bud.

For those few who have noticed and come to grips with the stark realities of deadly transfers in the global playground, the most common reaction has been to retreat into a private, protective "fortress" mentality. This stance is evidenced in behavior at several levels of analysis, as varied as the growth in gated communities which used armed guards to keep unwanted people out; the emergence of militia, vigilante, and survivalist groups who provide their own security with their own weaponry; and the resurgence of virulent nationalist movements (such as the "America first" movement in the United States and the "greater Serbia" movement in the former Yugoslavia) which seek to preserve their own lives and culture without regard for what happens elsewhere. The common thread running through these responses is a desire to protect oneself from an onslaught of danger and destruction, while presumably letting everyone else sink into the muck. The unstated premises here are a fatalistic acceptance that the society as a whole is falling apart, a cynicism that anything on a broad overarching level can be done to stop it, and thus a desperate, self-interested move to try to be one of the lucky ones who manages to survive and thrive in such an apocalyptic predicament.

It seems pretty clear that both those who deny the severity of the dangers of the global playground and those who respond to it by building walls around themselves are not helping to develop and spread a meaningful comprehension of the basic nature of the playground environment. Such an understanding appears essential as a prerequisite to any kind of effort to transform and improve this environment. While this study later examines the causes and consequences of the emergence of deadly transfers on the global playground, we need to know now a bit more about the principal players on the field. Figure 1 provides an integrated identification of the perpetrators, victims, and monitors.

THE UNRULY PERPETRATORS

Who are the bullies and ruffians on the global playground? It seems far too easy to label a single source as generating all of the problems here, as is all too common in the prevailing literature

Figure 1
Players on the Global Playground

THE UNRULY PERPETRATORS

Rogue States
Terrorist Groups
Criminal Organizations
Deviant Individuals

THE NOT-ALWAYS-INNOCENT VICTIMS

Largely Voluntary Victims	*Largely Involuntary Victims*
Corrupt Governments	Advanced Industrial Societies
Subversive Groups	Multinational Corporations
Greedy/Pleasure-Seeking Individuals	Wealthy/Powerful Individuals

INEFFECTIVE MONITORS

National Governments
International Organizations
Transnational Watchdog Groups

---

on the subject. Four distinct instigators operating internationally appear to shoulder the bulk of the responsibility here: rogue states, terrorist groups, criminal organizations, and deviant individuals. When the diversity of this set of perpetrators is combined with the recent expansion and diversification of the types of instruments they use and of the means of delivery,[1] the security threat becomes a paramount concern.

Rogue states, commonly identified as countries that shun civil participation in the international community (such as Iraq, Iran, Libya, and North Korea), seek to ignore any existing rules, to expand their own power, and to undermine the influence of the major powers. While in theory it might seems difficult to classify unruly actors within an anarchic system devoid of uniform rules, in practice it seems relatively easy to identify those extreme states that are both more flagrant and more destructive in their disregard for what little is left of overarching global norms of behavior. With the end to the Cold War and the global spread of democratic and capitalist values, these rogue states have by and large become even more marginalized—isolated and alienated—from the rest of the increasingly interconnected international system. The net result appears to be either to cause them to try to find ways to re-enter that system by abandoning their deviant practices or—far more likely given the nature of some of the ideologies involved—to become ever more determined to undermine the dominant global system. Many analysts agree that the threat from the rogue states, with their "military bullying" and "support for anti-government groups," is increasing in the 1990s.[2]

Terrorist groups, composed of desperate forces arrayed across national boundaries alienated from the dominant system, seek to achieve a variety of disruptive political ends through violence and threats of violence. While the particular methods utilized by terrorist groups have changed and expanded over time, the general approach of using the shock value of a particularly internationally abhorrent incident to capture public attention and further their cause has remained relatively constant. The emergence of the post–Cold War global playground appears particularly conducive to transnational terrorist activity because the combination of the promotion of free expression and the absence of coherent norms increases the potential perceived legitimacy of terrorist claims. The future for terrorism in this context appears to be quite bright: "terrorism's prospects, often overrated by the media, the public, and some politicians, are improving as its destructive potential increases" because of the rise of groups "that practice or might take up terrorism" (now expanded beyond the traditional terrorist profile to include disaffected religious, ethnic, and nationalist groups) and "the weapons available to them."[3]

Criminal organizations, coordinated more than ever as unified transnational forces refusing to follow existing regulations, seek illegal economic gain through a variety of coercive and salacious business activities. Local and national criminal syndicates ignore and violate state laws when they undertake their activities, and in many ways it is even easier for these organizations to ignore and violate the more poorly defined and less tightly enforced international laws in the open global environment. While natural tensions emerge when a criminal organization from one country begins to encroach on the turf of another country's organization, the specter of ever larger profits has generally led to a quickly agreed upon coordinated transnational arrangement providing both with more than they had before. Because "there is no economic incentive for transnational organized crime to diminish," it is "growing rapidly and represents a global phenomenon that is penetrating political institutions, undermining legitimate economic growth, threatening democracy and the rule of law, and contributing to the post-Soviet problem of the eruption of small, regionally contained, ethnic violence."[4]

Finally, deviant individuals, defined as those who reject the norms and rules of society, seek to escape from their depressing realities through illicit means such as psychoactive substances and violence without any regard about the consequences for themselves and others. While in the past unruly behavior on the global playground was largely the domain of large groups with substantial political and financial backing, in the future this behavior may very well become the province of "individuals or like-minded people working in very small groups, on the pattern of the technology-hating Unabomber"; a typical individual of this type may "possess the technical competence to steal, buy, or manufacture the weapons he or she needs," may espouse an ideology "even more aberrant than those of larger groups," and may be even more difficult to detect.[5] Deviant individuals are by far the least discussed and least predictable unruly players on the global playground.

The common theme running through these four sources is that each finds that it cannot fit into the prevailing society, becomes angry and frustrated about it, and rather than simply separating from the situation and isolating itself, decides to undertake unlawful activities that on the surface seem simply to satisfy its own desires but in reality end up wreaking havoc in the global community. While some of the four types of players delight in the chaos they create, others simply do not care and are concerned only about their own gratification and furthering their own cause. Due to the open structure of the global playground, each is able to continue and even expand its activities because its intentionally low-profile transnational behavior leads to a kind of immunity from prosecution.

In many ways, these unruly players on the global playground seem more aware of the true nature of their environment than anyone else. They understand well the differences between stated rules and actual practices, the circumstances under which they can engage in forbidden behavior and get away with it, the exact vulnerabilities of a system characterized by almost complete anarchy, and the ways of evading penalties if they are caught. They harbor no illusions that they are functioning in an orderly, civilized setting, and reasonably assume that many on the playground will choose to collude with them for private gain or ignore these disruptive players' behavior as long as it does not affect them directly. In other words, the unruly players feel completely at home in a playground atmosphere, for that is a setting that they feel is quite natural because it matches their own anarchic self-seeking predisposition.

Beyond mere understanding, the bullies and ruffians on the global playground know exactly how to make the most of the disorderly setting. For example, transnational criminal organizations flourish in situations characterized by "weak structures and dubious legitimacy," as "they take advantage of the chaos that exists" and seek to perpetuate "the crisis of governance and decline of civil society that have become familiar features of the post–Cold War world."[6] While the unruly players are not themselves responsible for the creation of the anarchy on the playground, they are much more savvy in exploiting it than existing authority structures are in managing it.

THE NOT-ALWAYS-INNOCENT VICTIMS

Who are the usual victims of this disruptive activity on the global playground? While the answer here is less clear-cut than with the initiators, a few patterns do stand out. There is an important distinction here between (1) voluntary victims who choose to receive what the bullies and ruffians are offering because these recipients think they are benefiting from it and (2) involuntary victims who the bullies and ruffians strip of power, protection, or property for their nefarious ends. Rogue states tend to go after advanced industrial societies—the so-called "civilized" states— and the integrity of the international system as a whole. Terrorist groups choose these same developed nations as their targets, where the shock value of their politically motivated violence is highest, as well as large multinational corporations that symbolize the same oppressive status quo power structure to them. Both rogue states and terrorist groups tend to support and inflame local insurgent groups seeking to disrupt governmental stability. Criminal organizations also aim at these wealthy corporations (as well as, of course, rich individuals), but they also prey on vulnerable, volatile individuals seeking quick escape from unfortunate situations (such as urban gangs, drug addicts, and undocumented aliens). Often the individuals criminal organizations attempt to seduce are influential government officials. Deviant individuals strike out at whatever and whoever stands in the way of their quest for gratification and expression of pent-up outrage. The overall trend here is that, with the exception of innocent bystanders who always bear a substantial proportion of the negative repercussions from the unruly perpetrators' disruptive behavior, the victims tend to be either those who represent the prevailing establishment and its norms or those who are disenfranchised elements of society who are highly vulnerable to the seductive appeal of the unruly players on the global playground.

Unlike the initiators, the victims on the global playground—particularly the involuntary ones—generally appear to have an inadequate understanding of the security setting in which they function. These victims express surprise and sometimes genuine shock when they end up as targets of unsanctioned behavior, even though an increasing number of those around them have been similarly victimized in the past. The establishment victims express anger and resentment that law enforcement institutions, both national and international, are not capable of preventing the abuses or at the very least immediately tracking down and apprehending the perpetrators, even though the success record in this prevention and apprehension has historically been consistently quite low. The disenfranchised victims look for scapegoats to rationalize their succumbing to the temptation to partake in the deadly transfers. The last thing many of the victims consider, whether they be established or disenfranchised, is the possibility that some of their own values and preferences (including their own promotion of individualistic self-gratification) may have contributed to their selection as targets, making them at least partially accountable for their plight. Many victims do not even realize what others have taken away from them because of the proliferation of ominous transnational flows—in a sense, we are all victims of these deadly transfers because of the constricted liberty and loss of freedom we all face now due to the pervasiveness of their activity.[7] In sum, these victims at least initially (after repeated offenses their attitudes usually change) cling to an ideal notion of how everything should function, refusing to adjust to the stark realities on the global playground that surround them.

The consequences of this shock and finger pointing are that these victims never seem able to extract themselves on their own from the negative impact of the ominous transnational flows. Like unwary individuals on school and park playgrounds, they have no ability to manage danger once it besets them precisely because they maintain a false confidence that the environment is safe, a false trust in the ability of the playground monitors to resolve any difficulties they encounter, or a fatalistic acceptance that serious harm is likely to befall them no matter what they do. In many ways, assuming a sense of full personal accountability and responsibility seems antithetical to the essence of a playground environment.

THE INEFFECTIVE MONITORS

Finally, who are the monitors on the global playground? National governments, international organizations, and transnational watchdog groups all are involved here. National governments possess the greatest coercive enforcement authority here through their internal police force and their external military force, but they face two major problems in confronting the playground's ruffians and bullies: detecting the unsanctioned behavior is quite difficult because it is most commonly undertaken covertly, and punishing such activity when detected is difficult due to the international scope of the perpetrators and due to the sympathy and collusion of many of these governments' own citizenry in the unlawful acts. International organizations such as the United Nations (UN) possess the most comprehensive global scope in their legitimate purview, but they lack any semblance of enforcement capabilities (notwithstanding the largely symbolic UN peacekeeping forces) and constantly are thwarted by national sovereignty concerns (parallel to the impediments posed by basic individual civil liberties on school and park playgrounds). Transnational watchdog groups possess the largest capacity to detect unruly activities, due in part to their connection to local grassroots monitoring efforts (Amnesty International is an excellent example here), but like the international organizations they lack enforcement powers and in addition they frequently lack the legitimacy to initiate proscriptive policies.

As might be expected, these monitors of the global playground stand in the middle between the savvy awareness of the initiators of the turmoil and the naïve ignorance of the victims. The monitors understand the anarchic setting and the pervasiveness of unsanctioned activities, and although they occasionally call for more monitors and monitoring devices deep down inside they know that this will not solve the problem. While some of the monitors have become quite jaded (such as authorities attempting to prevent the flow of drugs and illegal migrants across boundaries) about their potential effectiveness, it is crucial to realize that many harbor considerable hope that through concerted effort the unruly behavior can be dramatically reduced if not eliminated. When looking back at past failures, monitors emphasize new detection technologies or growing global consensus about banning these activities as evidence for this optimism for the future. However, the monitors do not expect rapid and dramatic improvement in the situation, so they call upon the victims to be patient and to understand more fully the complexities of stopping the unlawful global behavior.

In undertaking concerted action to restrain unruly behavior on the global playground, the monitors are still operating at a relatively preliminary and tentative level. Their basic thrust at this point appears to focus on spreading awareness of the pervasiveness of this unruly behavior by talking about it with each other, in the process developing common understandings of the problems, common clarification of norms, and common approaches to restoring order. Perhaps the most ambitious thrust has been the recent attempt to establish an International Criminal Court to bring those breaking the law to justice for crimes committed that are beyond the jurisdiction of any one nation-state: on June 15, 1998, delegates from over 150 nations met in Rome to begin negotiations on this issue.[8] However, the rather distinctive concerns of these states about protecting the rights of their own citizens pose a major stumbling block to this initiative, as they do to any effort to strengthen the collective power of the monitors on the global playground.

ANARCHY, SOVEREIGNTY, AND GLOBALIZATION

In the end, much of the chaos on the global playground is due to the clash among the competing pressures of anarchy, sovereignty, and globalization. The state of anarchy reflects the absence of overarching common norms and common meaningful authority structures on the international level, fostering a kind of "every-state-for-itself" mentality. The perpetuation of the notion of national sovereignty involves a continuing belief by nation-states that they should be able to have complete jurisdiction over what goes on within their boundaries, and that they should not have to undertake significant compromise in these state rights for the common good. Globalization introduces the notion that, due to the growing interdependence of states, each nation's actions will increasingly have international repercussions, and that as a result it makes the most sense to approach issues on a broad multilateral basis.

A major problem develops when combining these three trends, particularly in the specific context of deadly transfers on the global playground. When globalized threats emerge, national sovereignty can create a stubborn refusal to confront them in a concerted manner, and the prevailing sense of anarchy creates a fatalistic expectation that efforts to act jointly are doomed to failure in any case. When deadly transfers occur on the global playground, sovereignty concerns can stimulate an unwillingness to allow external officials to track down the perpetrators or to establish common rules across nations so that those involved in these ominous transnational flows face the same penalties no matter where they operate. The "dark underside" of globalization and interdependence is the way it so conveniently facilitates the movement of unsanctioned substance and people across national boundaries.[9] When the deadly transfers become globalized, operating in a similar way in many different parts of the world, anarchy plays a crucial role in preventing coordinated responses to these dangerous transactions. It is as if on school and park playgrounds the play area were divided up into several sectors, each with its own set of monitors operating according to a slightly different set of rules and enforcement mechanisms and refusing to cooperate much with each other when facing a common set of problems. The clear result of such a predicament is the ability of the perpetrators of the deadly transfers to move across sectors, finding the ones with the most distracted, inept, or corruptible monitors in which to operate. The initiators of these ominous transnational flows can then thrive and expand into effective international operations because their ability to overcome the rigidities of sovereignty, take advantage of the anarchic playground environment, and mirror the interdependent efficiencies of globalization is far greater than that of the playground monitors, particularly considering monitors which are nation-state governments.

Chapter 2

The Spread of
Deadly Transfers

Out of all the various activities that occur on the global playground, this study chooses to focus on deadly transfers, the ominous transnational flows that move largely without detection from place to place.[10] In a highly open and interdependent world, there appears to be an exceptionally high vulnerability to these dangerous flows, combined with an exceptionally low awareness of their pervasiveness and an exceptionally high level of perplexity about how to cope with them. An underlying premise of this study's emphasis is that in today's world, what passes among the various players on the world scene may be even more important than what occurs within them.

DEFINING DEADLY TRANSFERS

Delineating the scope of the deadly transfers that occur on the global playground is a bit tricky. A huge variety of people, technologies, and substances moves across boundaries in today's world, and this study purposely examines only a narrow subset of them. Several characteristics help to define the particular selection. The chosen transfers are transnational, because they consist of cross-boundary interactions largely among private groups (rather than national governments) and are far more likely to occur outside the norms and rules of the international system. The included flows are covert, as they are largely informal transactions that occur in secret, violating global norms or explicit national and international laws and invisible to international scrutiny. Finally, included flows are ominous in the sense that the dominant international community view is that they endanger in a major way national or international security, excluding both (1) positive transactions, such as many transfers of material wealth or constructive ideas, and (2) transactions without a sizable security impact, such as the transmission of stolen art or automobiles. The notion of security embedded here is a comprehensive one, still emphasizing the survival of state governments and national societies yet extending well beyond traditional political-military issues to encompass economic, cultural, and environmental concerns.[11]

The rationale for selecting this particular slice of global transactions reflects a desire to focus on the most severe challenges the nation-state faces regarding cross-border movement. The choice of transnational flows is due to the importance of analyzing transactions that governments can influence but not totally control, as in the post–Cold War context forces that are neither completely inside nor completely outside a state's purview merit particular attention. The emphasis on covert flows derives from the increasing opportunity in today's world for the frequent occurrence and damaging impact of transactions that consciously violate or circumvent the norms and rules of the international system, where coordinated, unsanctioned behavior has the potential to undermine system stability (even though monitors are generally inept, it is still often preferable to be on the safe side to transfer illicit substances covertly). Finally, dealing with the most ominous flows seems to be crucial in order to understand the way the international system perceives stress, attempts to respond to stress, and on occasion cracks under stress. Ultimately, a significant overarching underpinning for scrutinizing these ominous transnational flows is their tendency to highlight weaknesses in the nation-state system: they can provide an index of the permeability of national borders, displaying for all to see the extent to which national governments can control what moves across their boundaries; and they can serve as a lightning rod for the meaningfulness of the notion of world order, revealing whether or not it is just a pretense for considerable incoherence and paralysis in international policy and action.

When considering the full variety of security threats that emerge on the global playground, it should be relatively clear that ominous transnational flows are not the only form of dangerous behavior that occurs there. For example, if individuals come to the playground and begin shooting people with homemade arms (without transferring weapons to anyone), ingesting homegrown illicit drugs (without distributing them to anyone), or dumping their own toxic materials (without selling them to anyone), a major security threat emerges without the occurrence of a single deadly transfer. On the international level, a blatant instance of a major security threat without the involvement of ominous transnational flows would occur if a nation developed a nuclear bomb on its own (assuming, of course, that the components were not procured through the flow of hazardous materials).

However, this study contends that the deadly transfers across national boundaries deserve special attention because they involve a crucial contagion effect across parties. Through these ominous transnational flows the unsanctioned behavior of one individual, group, or nation extends to another individual, group, or nation; once the infrastructure is set up for cross-national transmission, the spread of these undesired activities accelerates even further. A confinable local or national security threat can quickly escalate to become an international threat on the global playground, making it all the more unstoppable. Moreover, in a highly interdependent world the state of international relations serves in many ways as a lightning rod for the degree of dysfunction within nations, just as on the playground the passing around of dangerous substances and technologies is a reflection of deep problems within the initiators of this activity. When dangerous cross-national transactions occur on a regular basis, it is a sign not only that governments and international organizations may be unable (or unwilling) to reign in such activity, but also that widespread individual attitudes condone this activity to a certain extent. In parallel fashion, a sharp reduction in deadly transfers would assuredly be a sign of significant improvement within the players on the global playground.

While the focus of deadly transfers selected for study is explicitly international in scope, it is important to note a difference between those transactions that occur within nations and those that occur across nations. When these ominous flows occur within nations, they pose a severe threat to domestic stability but do not involve the potentially illegitimate and certainly resented intrusion by alien parties into the internal affairs of a nation-state. In contrast, when these ominous flows occur across nations, the hostility and finger pointing associated with their foreign origin compound whatever disruption of internal stability occurs. Thus, although deadly transfers have a seemingly equal potential to escalate instability whether they occur outside or inside a nation, the overall pernicious implications are greater when these dangerous transactions cross state boundaries because of the perceived violation of national sovereignty and the reduced ability and responsibility felt by the victim to rectify the resulting problems created. For this reason, this study emphasizes the cross-national occurrence of the deadly transfers, while at the same time not excluding the internal transactions that clearly can and have taken a terrible toll on modern society.

Similarly, there is a crucial, underlying difference among the deadly transfers between those that are unintentional, composed of either human accidents or acts of God, and those that are intentional, which humans knowingly initiate. When a particular ominous transnational flow is unintentional, the damage may be huge but it is hard to assign blame for the negative consequences. In contrast, when such a flow is intentional, the local, national, and international community is quick to highlight the perpetrators—assuming that the initiating parties can be identified (which is certainly not always the case with the deadly transfers)—and hold them directly responsible for any problems that ensue. Moreover, due to this distinction, victim societies are much more likely to be fatalistic and accepting of transfers perceived as unintentional, with far fewer ripple effects in terms of anger and hostility, transnational tensions, and the potential for conflict. For this reason, this study emphasizes intentional deadly transfers while not excluding crucial, unintentional transactions that wreak havoc in the civilized world.

Based on the specified criteria, six deadly transfers appear deserving of special scrutiny in this study. These transfers cover clandestine conventional arms, illicit psychoactive drugs, illegal human migrants, unsanctioned hazardous materials (including both toxic waste and nuclear materials), lethal infectious diseases (including both the unintentional spread of deadly microbes and the intentional dissemination of dangerous biological agents), and incapacitating information disruptions. These ominous transnational flows together appear to create incredibly damaging problems that resist easy remedies on the global playground.

There is no underlying assumption of complete comprehensiveness here, encompassing every possible type of international transfer fitting the criteria for inclusion mentioned earlier in the chapter. For example, some might consider including transnational flows of fanatical extremist ideologies or intolerant "believe-or-die" religions and cults, but these reflect more the transmission of broad ideas (which are difficult to isolate in terms of their threat and whose spread falls well within the norms of the global system) rather than of specific, tangible, intrinsically dangerous, and explicitly outlawed items across national boundaries. Others might wish to include the cross-national spread of fear and panic often associated with severe economic downturns, but here we are dealing with concern about the contagious spread of setbacks occurring largely within states rather than about specific substances transmitted across states. Still others might be tempted to incorporate the illegal global traffic in stolen goods (across a broad range of commodities) or pornography, but these transnational flows do not seem to pose directly major security threats. It is thus a fundamental premise of this study that the six chosen deadly transfers represent the most important, immediate, and dangerous challenges to national and global security today. Figure 2 displays this selected set of transfers along with the primary direction of their movement and the primary nature of their disruptive impact.

THREATS POSED BY DEADLY TRANSFERS

Together these deadly transfers end up threatening three crucial protection goals: (1) basic biological survival, including preserving human life, natural resources needed to sustain life, and minimal thresholds of environmental quality within one's national territory; (2) fundamental political authority, including preserving the existing state regime in power and promoting the continuation of

Figure 2
Deadly Transfers on the Global Playground

Flow Identity	Primary Flow Direction	Primary Flow Disruption
Clandestine Arms	North to South	Political-Military Stability
Illegal Migrants	South to North	Civil Economic Norms
Illicit Drugs	South to North	Civil Social Norms
Hazardous Materials	North to South	Environmental Sustainability
Infectious Diseases	Mixed	Human Health
Information Disruptions	Mixed	Organizational Communication

its ideology; and (3) essential socioeconomic cohesion, including preserving long-standing cultural traditions and maintaining a minimum threshold of material wealth so that the social fabric is not ripped apart. These three goals relate closely to a commonly accepted taxonomy of what each state strives to safeguard through its national security policy.[12] In many senses, these three aspects of protection represent the principal areas where there is an overall security desire to preserve system stability. The flows of lethal infectious diseases and unsanctioned hazardous waste largely end up challenging biological survival; the flows of clandestine conventional arms and incapacitating information disruptions largely end up challenging political authority; and the flows of illicit psychoactive drugs and illegal human migrants largely end up challenging socioeconomic cohesion. Figure 3 displays a severity scale for each of the three domains of security protection threat associated with the deadly transfers.

Within each of the six ominous transnational flows, the greatest danger appears generally to emerge when organized groups rather than individuals or national governments control these transactions. Terrorist groups and criminal organizations, in particular, seem to convert flows that could have a minor isolated impact into ones that end up having national—and often system-wide—repercussions. The international transactions of these or-

Figure 3
Severity of Protection Threats from Deadly Transfers

	High	*Medium*	*Low*
Biological Survival	Kills people	Destroys natural environment	Endangers human health and habitat sustainability
Political Authority	Overthrows government	Interferes with government's ability to communicate and reduces its legitimacy	Distorts government's message or lowers its centrality
Socioeconomic Cohesion	Creates social and ethnic strife	Challenges social and economic practices	Increases social and economic burdens

ganized groups appear to be considerably harder to detect than those of rogue states, who after all have a much more fixed and limited geographical base for their nefarious activities. Deadly transfers undertaken by deviant individuals appear to have a more limited scope and a lower probability for a rapid contagion effect than do those undertaken by organized groups.

While all transfers of clandestine arms across borders in some way threaten biological survival, transferring them into the hands of organized groups—including insurgent groups and street gangs as well as terrorist groups and criminal organizations—seems to make the ramifications of the violence more likely to threaten political authority and socioeconomic cohesion than if these weapons are just randomly scattered among the population at large. With illegal migrants, smuggling operations by transnational criminal organizations seem to make the consequences of this people movement much more damaging to the political authority and socioeconomic cohesion of both sending and receiving states than if the unauthorized aliens come in on their own (because these smuggling operations have developed an organized effective system for subverting authority, rather than simply slipping through random holes in a protective security net). With illicit drugs, the control by transnational criminal organizations seems to be at the heart of what makes the attempt to escape from reality so destructive to socioeconomic cohesion in the recipient countries. With hazardous materials, the greatest security threat seems to be posed by the transfer of nuclear components to transnational terrorist groups, as opposed to the transfer of conventional waste to greedy individual entrepreneurs. With infectious diseases, most people would seem to experience greater panic if a transnational terrorist group intentionally spread a lethal biological agent such as anthrax in a major city than if an unintended outbreak of an infectious parasitic disease occurred. Finally, with information disruptions, organized group efforts to bring down an entire defense or business information system seem to be much more deadly than individual hackers' experimentation to see if they can break into a secure system just to demonstrate their cleverness.

The deadly transfers flow in different directions internationally, making it impossible to point to one geographical source or one type of nation as primarily responsible. Clandestine arms and hazardous materials flow mainly from the North to the South, as industrialized nations have excess weapons capacity and excess toxic waste, and the developing states still have a lot of internal turmoil and desire to make money, even involving lethal materials. Illegal migrants and illicit drugs flow principally from the South to the North, as people from deprived countries seek to flee from poverty, war, and oppression and people in wealthy countries seek to indulge in psychoactive stimulation. Infectious diseases and information disruptions appear to flow in both directions, as lethal microbes and biological agents have originated in both the North and the South and savvy disruptive hackers can operate (and have operated) from anywhere in the world. So stereotypical accusations of "major power imperialism" or the "threat from below" both appear to be groundless as a universal means of characterizing the deadly transfers. Nevertheless, the huge and growing global gap in wealth and power between the "haves" and "have-nots" appears to bear a considerable portion of the responsibility for the frequency of these unsanctioned cross-national transactions and their destructive impact, as well as for the sense of fear associated with them.[13] Indeed, there is considerable reason to believe that ethnocentric and even racist impulses may be involved in the deadly transfers moving from North to South, and that the severe poverty levels in the Third World may serve to exacerbate the impact of the ominous flows which end up there.

The six flows considered in this study are highly interrelated. On the surface, it seems that the flow of clandestine conventional arms stimulates strictly political-military threats, the flows of illegal human migrants and illicit psychoactive drugs stimulate strictly socioeconomic threats, the flow of incapacitating information disruptions stimulates strictly communication threats, and the flows of unsanctioned hazardous materials and toxic infectious diseases stimulate strictly human health and natural environment threats. But the interactions are more complex than this, and to isolate the relationship between flows and threats in this artificially compartmentalized way would be to fall into the same trap as those who analyze each of the threats in isolation from the rest.

While depicting the entire web of potential interconnections would be too cumbersome, it is worth highlighting the overarching patterns involved. A few anecdotal examples of the more direct links seem useful to illustrate these interconnections: the profits made from the sale of illicit drugs have often fueled the purchase of covert arms to be used in insurgency or terrorist activities;[14] environmental degradation linked to hazardous waste flows has on more than one occasion led to the creation of outflows of illegal migrants seeking better habitats;[15] information disruptions can lead to a breakdown of military command-and-control systems managing conventional weaponry;[16] the use of illicit drugs may lead to hazardous waste flows, as for example Andean waterways now show signs of serious pollution from cocaine refining;[17] the spread of hazardous materials can and has led to epidemics of infectious diseases; illegal aliens entering a country may serve as vehicles for transporting illicit drugs across borders undetected;[18] and the use of conventional weapons (often those procured covertly) in regional warfare can often accelerate the creation of hazardous waste.[19] Current trends suggest that the deadly transfers are indeed becoming even more intertwined over time.

The pattern of linkage between the deadly transfers and their perpetrators is also complex. Rogue states and terrorist groups have been very much involved in the flow of clandestine conventional arms and have shown a great future potential to be involved in the flow of lethal infectious diseases (through spreading toxic biological agents) and in the flow of incapacitating information disruptions (through finding ways to bring down targeted communications systems); criminal organizations are involved in the flows of clandestine arms, illicit psychoactive drugs, illegal human migrants, unsanctioned hazardous materials, and incapacitating information disruptions; and deviant individuals, the least predictable of the players here, can be involved in any of the ominous transnational flows. The difference between the largely politically-driven terrorist groups and the largely economically-driven criminal groups is noteworthy: the former use the deadly transfers largely to bring down governments and to undermine status quo structures, while the latter use them largely to reap huge profits and to become part of status quo structures.

In the end, what is perhaps most disconcerting is that as the web of interconnections among the deadly transfers and the web of linkages between the deadly transfers and their perpetrators both become tighter and more multifaceted, it becomes increasingly difficult to detect who is doing what and to decide where to begin in any attempt to manage the chaotic predicament. From the point of view of the playground monitors, it would be a lot nicer if each type of dangerous transaction derived from a single type of bully or ruffian; if this were true, then a discrete sequential solution to each ominous flow could proceed handily. Unfortunately, the predicament instead is gradually transforming in such a way as to make effective management more remote.

Chapter 3

Intractable Causes, Pernicious Consequences, and Futile Cures

Too often it seems that analysts plunge into colorful descriptions of ominous transnational flows moving across national boundaries without providing any general understanding of the broad context within which these dangerous transactions operate.[20] The aftermath of the Cold War's demise in 1989 has left a rather peculiar international security setting, one in which deadly transfers prosper, pose major threats, and promote failure for any proposed remedies. This setting involves not only widely discussed changes in system structures but also equally important, often ignored changes in individual attitudes. Comprehending the dire nature of this predicament is an essential prerequisite to any attempt to transform the chaotic anarchy of today's global playground.

INTRACTABLE CAUSES OF DEADLY TRANSFERS

While deadly transfers have occurred across human societies for ages, the post–Cold War context has been uniquely conducive to a mushrooming of these ominous transnational flows. The nature of the changes in system structure and individual attitudes has made the global arena almost ideal for these transactions. The deep and multifaceted roots of this international predicament have made it difficult for either national governments or the mass public to get a handle on why things have changed for the worse so rapidly.

The precipitants of these flows related to system structure have been the most commonly discussed because the openness of the current global environment has appeared to foster a nearly universal vulnerability to the deadly transfers. First, the rapid advances in transportation and communication (including the accelerating development of information technologies) have led to a huge increase in the volume of international transactions; and with this growth in trade, investment, and travel, those seeking to move covertly illegal people and products across national boundaries can easily hide in the mass of legitimate travelers and commodities.[21] There are more transmission points than ever before, and national borders have become truly porous. Internationally accepted norms prevent substantial long-term curtailing of the principle of open movement of goods and people from place to place.

Second, the increasing number and power of transnational nongovernmental groups has stimulated these covert flows; those involved in facilitating these transfers seem to be bound together by a desire to attack the rule of law "either to destroy it or (as in more recent times) to change it radically."[22] Motivated by the passionate interests of their members and able to coordinate and publicize their purposes as never before, they become global "special-interest" groups that ignore general global welfare except as it relates to their own agenda. National governments have increasingly watched issues outside of their own narrow sovereign territories fall under the influence of these groups, who in many ways know better than states how to operate effectively on a global scale.

Third, heightened global interdependence and the increasing responsiveness of the global marketplace to expressed material desires play a major role here. International interdependence has, of course, existed for some time, including during the Cold War, when there was a kind of forced interdependence within each of the two bipolar blocs. However, the kind of interdependence that is widespread today, accelerated by the growing transportation and communication systems and transnational organizations, is complex and "multilevel,"[23] preventing any single actor from having the ability to alter it or break out of it. If a surplus develops in the supply of weapons, as occurred after the end of the Cold War, or an increased demand occurs for illicit drugs, as has been the case in recent years, then the globally interdependent market is quick to respond by facilitating transactions virtually no matter what kinds of objections any single country may have.

Turning to precipitants of the deadly transfers related to individual attitudes, the emphasis on freedom and individualism has had a major role to play. In particular, the international spread of liberal democratic beliefs, including support (especially at the rhetorical level) for free movement of goods and people across boundaries, has substantially lessened the capacity of border police to detect and restrict surreptitious flows across countries;[24] the earlier presence during the Cold War of police states with their informants and tight monitoring had made such transactions considerably more difficult.[25]

A second attitudinal influence on the spread of deadly transfers revolves around an "escape-from-reality" syndrome. While in many ways people have grown more fatalistic about increased threat and incivility in society as a whole, ironically on an individual level they have become less tolerant of failure, disappointment, and any hardships they suffer. While apathy may well be the primary societal mode of dealing with current global stress, allowing ominous flows to pass largely unnoticed from place to place, there still appear to be individuals and small groups that are unable to ignore the widespread state of societal dysfunction. These societal "losers" frequently become alienated and angry, searching for a scapegoat for their problems and all too ready to disrupt or overturn hierarchies they see as oppressive and stifling as an outlet for their tensions. As a result, if things do not go well they seem quicker to want to disconnect from their predicament by moving away (legally or illegally), taking drugs, acquiring weapons and engaging in violence (we have recently witnessed individual acts of mass violence triggered by as little as loss of a girlfriend or job or expulsion from school), or in other ways insulating themselves from the anguish of having to confront directly the mess which they themselves have created. This desire to escape from reality, often by altering one's consciousness in a way that numbs these negative sensations, has been achieved by a variety of means throughout human history;[26] what is distinctive today is the global pervasiveness of this pattern and its more direct linkage to security concerns.

Finally, a closely related individual attitude facilitating deadly transfers is the increasing focus on immediate material self-gratification at the expense of a sense of broad civic responsibility: as historian William McNeill colorfully puts it, "the glorification of instant gratification of personal impulse as the presumed path to happiness and success" is an "essentially adolescent" ideal, and "its principal defect is that it undermines human solidarities by putting personal wishes and demands ahead of any sort of obligation to others."[27] This widely discussed trend has been attributed to many sources, including television, the Internet, video games, and family breakdown; but regardless of its origins the result has been a loss of patience, an emphasis on fulfilling one's own desires right away, and a deterioration of the feeling of connection, caring, and responsibility for other people. While hedonistic behavior can certainly occur safely and privately on an individual level and not threaten overall security, the growing ethic of immediate self-gratification does appear to link in a direct and substantial way to damaging decay in protective authority structures on all levels. It is easy to see how this attitude could be highly conducive to deadly transfers, as people would increasingly not want to wait for legal or safe means of obtaining what they want.

Behind these structural and attitudinal precipitants of deadly transfers, some festering underlying tensions are evident. One of the basic dilemmas that is immediately apparent is that engaging in these ominous transnational flows brings large, tangible short-term benefits to the initiators (and often also to the recipients), but at the same time contains significant, less-visible long-term costs to society (and the international system) as a whole. When this unfortunate state of affairs is combined with the reality that most deadly transfers are either undetectable or perceived as undetectable, the incentive system favoring the spread of these pernicious flows becomes crystal clear. In situations where the attractiveness of individual satisfaction competes against the guilt arising from the global burdens created, there appears to be little question which would win in a system dominated by modern values.

PERNICIOUS CONSEQUENCES OF DEADLY TRANSFERS

The ending of the Cold War context has also led to the deadly transfers having particularly dangerous consequences on global society. Once again, transformations both in system structure and in individual attitudes have played a major role in determining the nature of these impacts from the flows on the global playground. These flows appear inescapably to involve impacts that are not readily confinable, involving considerable contagion within and across states. As is often the case, these outcomes are a lot easier to see than the roots of the deadly transfers or the transfers themselves, so that many onlookers do not connect the pernicious patterns observed with deadly transfers and instead attribute them to other kinds of causes.

Deadly transfer outcomes associated with system structure involve the gradual disintegration of global order. First, there has been a dramatic rise in violence of both the premeditated organized and sporadic random varieties.[28] Rapid international change helps to facilitate an international environment in which transfers of weapons and drugs know no established boundaries and often entail murder as a routine part of daily operations. The emphasis on immediate gratification and the urgent need to escape from reality reduce any serious consideration of the long-range consequences of violent actions by the perpetrators involved.

Second, these ominous transnational flows can result in the loss of civil society. The long-standing notion of civil society involves a sense of social contract between the ruler and the ruled and among the citizenry of a country that prohibits behavior that unduly interferes with the rights of others or that in any other way violates the principles of justice. The anarchic nature of deadly transfers leads to their increasing intrusion into these relationships in such a way as to reduce a respect for others' rights, to distort the basic sense of justice (often a "might makes right" mentality emerges), and to reduce the likelihood that civil discourse will be the route chosen for resolving disagreements. Any existing moral consensus begins to erode, as the ominous transnational flows often relate to cloudy ethical areas reflecting tensions between fulfilling the desires of the populace and reinforcing social order. The basis for this erosion can be a systemic confusion about societal values, involving not only uncertainty surrounding the rights of individuals and states but ambiguity about the rights of subnational and transnational groups.[29] As deadly transfers spread, those involved in these dangerous transactions are viewed as less deviant, and each member of the global society begins to question why it should abide by civilized rules when it seems that everyone else does not.

Another aspect of this loss of civil society involves the breakdown of the state. Deadly transfers appear to accelerate the contraction of governmental ability to provide for the needs of the citizenry, causing the very basis for the existence of government to diminish. Because the motives of those responsible for these flows often involve economic profit, the transmitters of the ominous flows tend to ignore the interests of the population at large and can undermine national and international regime stability.[30]

Finally, a third structural outcome of deadly transfers is to increase the likelihood that internal security threats may overshadow external ones. In a sense, the spread of externally induced disruption within states through these flows makes advanced industrialized nations more like Third World countries, who have traditionally had to focus on internal security concerns.[31] One of the more indirect consequences of these ominous transnational flows fostering internal insecurity is to increase the gap between the rich and the poor within societies: generally wealth moves to those involved in initiating the deadly transfers, while the remainder of society ends up paying more in terms of both (1) coping with the havoc wreaked by these transactions and (2) dealing with the specter of increased cost and decreased quality of goods and services.

Moving to the consequences of deadly transfers linked to individual attitudes, perhaps the most central impact is an increased sense of vulnerability on the part of the people and, less visibly, on the part of the government officials themselves. As the realization spreads that these ominous transnational flows are so pervasive and undetectable that no public or private security system can provide a firm shield against their pernicious impact, it becomes necessary to grapple with a sense of permanent fear due to permanent exposure to danger. Again, those who are well off or live in advanced industrial societies are most unused to this prospect and most unnerved by it.

A second dominant resulting individual attitude is the growth of cynicism and distrust. Fueled by the pervasiveness of deadly transfers, this distrust deepens both among citizenry, as one's own neighbor could be involved in these flows, and between citizens and their governments, as formal ruling bodies seem incapable of stopping these flows (and may, in the eyes of the populace, be tacitly involved as well). Many citizens may begin to question why they should support government when it cannot provide them with basic security, and (as alluded to earlier) there is little understanding of or sympathy toward the plight governments face in formulating effective policy to stop the deadly transfers.

Finally, the sense of vulnerability and distrust combine to stimulate the spread of a xenophobic "fortress mentality" among government officials and the public at large. Referred to in Chapter 1 as a typical reaction among those sensing the presence of a global playground, this attitude no longer permits inclusion of the broad concerns of others because of its most basic assumption that only a few lucky members of global society will survive unscathed by the direct and indirect ravages of the deadly transfers. Because one's fellow citizen seems untrustworthy, and because one's government seems helpless, there appears to be no other option besides providing one's own security as best one can without any reliance on others.

These structural and attitudinal consequences of deadly transfers highlight a couple of crucial underlying tensions. First, the increased visibility of the pursuit of power, pleasure, and wealth by both initiators and recipients of these flows creates a clash between stated sanctions and tangible material rewards. In other words, because it is so easy to see both the gains of those who indulge in the flows and the ineffectiveness of existing laws prohibiting these activities, onlookers can see a major disconnect between ideals and reality. Second, the consequences of the deadly transfers in many ways drive a wedge between concerns about economic profit and concerns about political security. In order to pursue successfully the societally-approved goal of accumulating wealth, it seems to many to become necessary (due to the lure of the ominous but profitable transnational flows) to engage in activities that ultimately sacrifice personal (and national) safety.

FUTILE CURES FOR DEADLY TRANSFERS

Society has not stood by idly watching deadly transfers spread on the global playground. Many remedies have been suggested or even applied on the local, national, and international levels to try to halt these flows in their tracks. Unfortunately, all have experienced futility in actually succeeding in curing the problem, and some have even had counterproductive backfire effects. With the widespread ineffectiveness of these measures largely matching pessimistic international expectations, there has been little detailed analysis of the pattern of futility here. Rather than presenting an in-depth review of each proposed or implemented solution, this section analyzes the system structural responses and individual attitudinal responses in a broader way so as to highlight some of the major obstacles impeding the success of any curative approach. Because the causes and consequences of the deadly transfers are so complex, dispersed, and interwoven, it should not be surprising here that public policy toward them has largely been barking up the wrong tree.

Systemic structural responses to deadly transfers have generally either proved to be cosmetic or made matters worse. Perhaps the most intuitive reaction to the ominous transnational flows is to pass national and international laws banning these activities; but, given the nature of the dangerous transactions, this legal action usually simply pushes the outlawed activity further underground, even when the regulations are accompanied by appropriate enforcement. When this happens, the transfers become harder to detect and are more likely to end up under transnational criminal control. Sadly, governments and international organizations often feel that the flow problem is resolved if such regulations exist, and subsequently they no longer track as much ominous cross-national activity, ignoring in the process the huge increase in black market transactions.

An opposite legal approach that some countries have seriously considered as a way of managing the deadly transfers is legalization, bringing these cross-national transactions into the accepted range of legitimate activities in the global society. With illicit drugs, clandestine arms, and illegal migrants the most widely discussed transactions here, many analysts feel that through legalization governments can be more effective in monitoring the transnational flows and in disconnecting these transactions from the ominous control of the unruly members of the global playground—rogue states, terrorist groups, criminal organizations, and deviant individuals. According to libertarian logic, a legalized "open-borders" policy would permit efficient global market forces to regulate properly these international flows. Beyond this general defense, special justifications for legalization exist for each of the affected deadly transfers: for illicit drugs, legalization is supposed to increase safety in drug use and prevent the spread of disease; for clandestine arms, legalization is supposed to help oppressed subnational groups protect themselves; and for illegal migrants, legalization is supposed to redistribute global population in a stabilizing manner that much more closely matches individual desires.

The difficulty here, as past evidence suggests perhaps most clearly when looking at tobacco and alcohol, is that by accepting the ominous transnational flows as legitimate activities well within the norms of the international system, these dangerous transactions are likely to proliferate in highly uneven (and unpredictable) ways, becoming even more deeply woven into the fabric of interaction within and across societies. While some deadly transfers may be deemed by parts of society to be less immediately harmful than others, the seemingly inevitable connections among the deadly transfers and among the types of unsavory distributors involved (even if the transactions were legal) makes it difficult to claim that there would be little overall negative impact on society. Economic supply and demand forces appear unlikely to create a global pattern of cross-national transactions that serves the needs of state security. There is no guarantee that increased monitoring possible through legalization will end up enhancing safety, helping the needy, or improving global distribution of goods and services.

A response to these deadly transfers similar to passing legislation yet in some ways even less effective is the initiation of global conferences on the various flows where most nations who attend sign tentative and usually non-binding agreements signaling their willingness to ban the ominous flows. This appears to be a symbolic, cosmetic "feel-good" solution to the problem, with absolutely no commitment to change behavior that facilitates or directly promotes these transactions: everyone leaves the conference smiling and shaking hands over what they have accomplished, but afterwards the deadly transfers usually continue unabated. Even worse, because most global conferences deal with only one of the ominous transnational flows, the crucial links among them remain unaddressed and largely misunderstood. Like the passage of law, this reaction can be worse than nothing because it may cause people to feel that they have effectively managed the problem and therefore do not need to attend to it any more.

On a national level, the parallel to these conferences is for governments to create new bureaucratic agencies whose specific responsibility is to manage some or all of the deadly transfers. While most of these transfers create organizational confusion because they span the mandates of existing governmental units, creating new agencies can end up even further complicating the ability to respond to quickly emerging problems related to these ominous flows (for example, turf battles may readily ensue). As with the international conferences, the agencies tend to deal with just one set of transactions rather than the interrelationships among them, and it seems that the primary purpose and impact of creating these agencies is cosmetic—to signal the citizenry that the government does indeed care and is trying to do something about the problem, even if no forward progress results from their creation.

Another common structural response to the ominous transnational flows is to address the supply rather than the demand end of the problems involved. Whether one is dealing with clandestine arms, illicit drugs, illegal migrants, hazardous materials, biological agents spreading infectious diseases, or information disruption systems, it is usually a whole lot more automatic to try to cut off the supply of unsanctioned people, technologies, and substances than it is to reduce the demand for them among alienated, greedy, or angry members of the global community. Unfortunately, focusing on the supply alone can only rarely significantly affect deadly transfers because (as mentioned earlier) in today's open society, as long as there are countries, groups, or individuals who really want outlawed commodities and technologies, the market will openly or secretly find ways of satisfying that demand.

Finally, by far the most direct structural cure aimed at the deadly transfers is the raw use of physical force—in the form of military coercion undertaken unilaterally or multilaterally—designed both to halt existing unsanctioned transactions and to deter future activities of this sort. While unruly players on the global playground certainly understand and respond to the direct use of force against them—indeed, some would argue that this is all they understand—the use of deterrence in this particular context faces some fundamental problems. To begin with, it has been widely accepted that the changes in the post–Cold War environment have dramatically reduced the effectiveness of classic deterrence[32] because of the breakdown of moral consensus and a universal signaling system to communicate overwhelming restraining force, the growth in the number and variety of new players in international relations, and the subtle nature of the activities that appear to be violating the status quo and require special sanctioning. Deterrence works best when there is an unambiguous threat, a readily identifiable aggressor, direct means to confront the threat, and superior power on the part of the deterring party to restrain or stop the rambunctious threat initiator, and these conditions rarely apply to today's anarchic security environment.

When one considers applying deterrence specifically to deadly transfers on the global playground, the obstacles to success become even larger. These ominous flows are initiated by disparate forces that are frequently dispersed internationally, making them quite difficult to pin down, apprehend, and punish; the interconnectedness among both these flows and their perpetrators can ironically make isolating the specific perpetrators of a particular transfer even more elusive. If one cannot ascertain with considerable certainty that a particular source is responsible for a deadly transfer, then deterrence is largely ineffective. The threat communicated by these transfers is often quite indirect, creating considerable ambiguity about the level of danger involved. Most importantly, as with attempts to curtail international terrorism in general, the application or threatened application of superior force as a means of stopping undesired activity not only usually fails to do so but also in many cases actually intensifies the resolve of the belligerent parties involved to continue and even escalate the unlawful behavior.

In contrast to these structural reactions, individual attitudinal responses about managing the deadly transfers have not played much of a role in policy makers' strategies for countering the spread of these ominous transnational flows. Indeed, the futility of the cures pursued by national governments can be explained at least in part by their insistence on viewing the whole problem with these dangerous transactions in a top-down "billiard-ball" manner, in a similar fashion to the way they would deal with an external enemy invading their borders. Because the deadly transfers fundamentally involve both initiating and targeting at the level of the mass public, understanding and taking into account its reactions to these ominous flows appears crucial. However, the dominant reaction of most countries' citizenry to managing the deadly transfers appears not to be particularly helpful in addressing these ominous transnational flows, as it is generally characterized by considerable paralysis, division, and abdication of responsibility.

Dealing first with this abdication of responsibility, the most important starting point for understanding individual attitudes about managing deadly transfers is to realize that the mass public does not believe that it is in any way accountable for helping to reduce these dangerous transactions. There appears to be a widespread stubborn refusal to recognize the tradeoff between immediate gratification of desires and social order, and along with this resistance there seems to be an unwillingness to abstain from activities that are directly or indirectly linked to the ominous transnational flows. In other words, as with many other security concerns, individuals, groups, and nations are willing to take a hard line toward these transactions as long as it entails absolutely no change in their lifestyles and standard mode of operations. In order to deflect attention away from this rigid blind spot, there is an awful lot of finger pointing and scapegoating surrounding the deadly transfers, reflecting claims that someone else is responsible for generating the problem and consequently that these others should be the ones forced to change.

Moving to the divided reactions to these transactions, it is quite clear that, despite the dangerous threat posed, no consensus in public opinion exists about how to manage the deadly transfers. More specifically, a gap exists between those emphasizing individual freedom and those emphasizing collective responsibility. An increasing number of members of society personally benefit monetarily from the ominous flows, so of course they would be opposed to any attempt to restrict them; and a segment of every society takes the free-market assumptions to their logical extreme by suggesting that it is wrong in principle to restrain the intentional human-initiated movement or any substance, technology, or person across national boundaries.

Finally, in contemplating management of the deadly transfers, members of the mass public and individual government officials often feel somewhat paralyzed. A widespread feeling of impotence permeates attitudes here because it is difficult to get a handle on where and how to begin effectively. As mentioned earlier, the intertwined transnational nature of these transactions makes atomistic, neatly segmented solutions to the problems associated with the ominous flows. The difficulties of monitoring the transfers and of differentiating them from perfectly acceptable cross-national transactions makes it difficult for most people even to get a realistic idea of the scope of the problem. So a feeling of "shooting-in-the-dark" often stands in the way of forward movement.

These structural and attitudinal responses to managing the deadly transfers clearly reflect a couple of underlying tensions. First, a pervasive reluctance exists about having open discussions between governments and their citizenry about the widening threat of the ominous flows and possible restrictive policies to address this threat; this reluctance seems to be largely due to fears about igniting the flames of internal divisiveness, about exposing government failures to manage the problem, or about triggering a mass panic about the breakdown of society. Second, all the incentives seem to point in the direction of taking piecemeal, flow-specific solutions largely directed at someone else, while what is really needed are holistic, systemic solutions significantly affecting everyone's behavior. To put it simply, the tendency here to take the easy way out, by not directly discussing the issues in a public forum and by not taking an overarching perspective on the flows tying them together, serves in the end to perpetuate the futility of cures addressed at the deadly transfers.

Chapter 4

Clandestine Arms Flows

The clandestine transfer of arms across national boundaries is per-haps the most long-standing security problem discussed in this study.[33] Placed in the context of the global playground, this covert global weapons traffic provides the means by which the ruffians and bullies maintain their disruptive power. Possessing no inher-ent legitimacy in the eyes of onlookers, these unruly players have to use instruments of violent force to have any sizable impact on their surroundings. With none of the know-how, resources, or technology needed to create these instruments themselves, the un-ruly players have to find ways to get weapons from other sources, fostering transfers in this area. Because officially sanctioned sources of arms would usually not sell to these unruly players, and because these players often do not have the capacity to com-pensate these sellers appropriately, the transactions that occur are often secret and illegal. In the most general terms, these arms transfers frequently constitute the devices enabling most of the other transfers discussed in this study to become truly deadly.

SCOPE OF THE PROBLEM

This ominous transnational flow includes conventional weapons components as well as finished conventional weapons systems, with the focus being on small arms and light weapons. Although major weapons systems "dwarf the capacities" of these arms, "hundreds of millions of low-tech, inexpensive, sturdy, easy-to-use weapons are the tools for most of the killing in contemporary conflicts—causing as much as 90 percent of the deaths."[34] Both black market and gray market transactions occur here: black market transfers directly violate relevant laws and usually involve weapons improperly obtained from government arsenals or legitimate arms dealers, while gray market transfers are more ambiguous legally and may involve either "dual-use" products shipped to recipients ineligible for military arms or government-sponsored transfers that violate existing prohibitions.[35] The international black market in arms, heavily involving transnational criminal organizations, frequently involves "the barter of weapons for natural resources, animal products, drugs, and other commodities."[36]

While the exact dollar amount of these covert flows is unknown, "guesses range from $1 billion–$2 billion for the average year's skullduggery (mostly by governments that do not want their neighbors to know what weapons they are buying or selling), to $5 billion–10 billion if there is a good war or two to drive demand."[37] This figure is of course substantially lower than the public international transfers of large conventional weapons systems ($18.5 billion in 1992), but the clandestine traffic is more likely to involve the kind of small arms actually used in ongoing conflicts and shows no signs of abating.[38] If one were to include both covert (unsanctioned) and overt (sanctioned) transfers, a 1998 estimate indicates that "$3 billion worth of small arms and light weapons are being shipped across international borders each year," "equivalent to about one-eighth of all international arms sales."[39] Another 1998 report indicates that "about a third of the small arms trade is 'illicit,' " with suppliers directly violating some existing law.[40]

RECENT HISTORY

The recent history of these clandestine arms flows (which are sometimes part of more broadly based covert operations) reveals that while they posed only minor problems for national governments during the early decades after World War II, by the mid-1970s the growing competition among supplying companies increased the volume of available munitions and made black market transactions—particularly in light weaponry—harder to control.[41] During the 1980s control eroded still further, as covert exchanges began to involve both light and heavy weapons and as governments themselves became more involved in clandestine arms flows, evidenced by arms scandals during that decade in the United States, France, Sweden, Austria, and Italy.[42] The proliferation of new primary suppliers, the breakdown of the regulatory structure, and the increasing market penetration of secondary suppliers of weapons and weapons components soon became embedded in a complex, multifaceted "international underground economy" managing the global distribution of all sorts of illegal commodities; this predicament has led to "a virtually impenetrable network of commercial and financial fronts behind which all manner of contraband deals—including arms shipments—can be conducted."[43]

More specifically, since 1980 there has been a greater worldwide demand for weapons obtained outside of normal channels, a shift away from bilateral national dealings in favor of arms bazaars (in the form of proliferating international military equipment exhibitions), a growing emphasis on spare parts (which are easier to obtain illegally), an increasingly prominent role for private arms dealers, and a tightening connection between the clandestine supply network for the drug trade and the arms trade.[44] The root causes for the increase in clandestine arms transfers during the 1980s include the increased international arms production during that decade and the growing obstacles facing any effort to control commercial exports.[45] The boom in legitimate arms traffic during that decade made arms transfers of any sort likely to be perceived as a much more routine commodity exchange.

After the end of the Cold War, "many observers breathed a sigh of relief that the winding down of the bipolar ideological rivalry would finally curtail the widespread development and exchange of potentially lethal weapons systems."[46] On the surface, the diminishing global demand for legitimately traded arms since the end of the Cold War,[47] with levels in the 1990s significantly lower than the 1970s and 1980s, seemed to fulfill their hopes. Much to their chagrin, however, excess supply of arms and excess capacity in arms production, combined with greater visibility of subnational turmoil, has fostered intensified competition by arms producers to enter foreign markets. It appears that the robust international weapons infrastructure stimulated by the 1980s boom refused to wither in the face of what might be perceived as a temporary downturn in arms demand.

Considerable confusion has surrounded who is initiating the covert post–Cold War arms transfers. The considerable finger pointing by major power governments about the unsavory sources spreading these weapons may be misguided: "although governments may profess concern about private arms smugglers and 'rogue' suppliers such as insurgent groups and drug traffickers, they themselves are by far the most important source of these weapons."[48] With the Cold War over, the armies of these major powers are shrinking, so they have given away or sold cheaply lots of non-state-of-the-art weapons to other countries; these arms filter "far beyond armies and police forces to opposition groups, criminal organizations, private security forces, vigilante squads, and individual citizens."[49] This pattern seems to erode any potential for credibility of major power arms control initiatives: as former Assistant Secretary of Defense Laurence Korb points out, "it is a frightening trend that undermines our moral authority in the New World Order" and makes it "very hard for us to tell other people—the Russians, the Chinese, the French—not to sell arms, when we are there peddling and fighting to control the market."[50]

Furthermore, questions surround the expectations of benefits by recipients of these arms transfers. While weapons transactions have traditionally been perceived as ways for new states, subnational ethnic separatists, or other somewhat disenfranchised groups to "assert their sovereignty,"[51] in practice the global arms trade today remains dependency generating.[52] It is indeed fascinating that the recipients of international weapons flows often continue to exaggerate the benefits of such arms acquisition, as for example "states that wish to assume a higher regional or global profile often assume that military prowess is the means of advancement, irrespective of whether or not the weapons are acquired to meet a definable threat in a militarily appropriate fashion."[53] In an era where economic growth appears to mean more to the international community than military might, this wishful thinking about arms transfers seems particularly inappropriate.

While undoubtedly much covert arms dealing remains undocumented, a few notorious cases serve to illustrate the wide range of parties involved. Perhaps the most well-known case is the Iran-Contra arms scandal, in which American government officials secretly sanctioned the sale of weapons to Iran in 1985–1986 in an attempt to secure the release of American hostages, with the funds received used in defiance of Congress to buy arms for Contra rebels in Nicaragua.[54] However, for the United States during the 1980s this was by no means an isolated incident: in 1983–1984 a couple of American businessmen shipped 87 state-of-the-art Hughes helicopters to the officially arms-embargoed North Korea;[55] and through most of the decade clandestine weapons aid flowed from the United States to Afghanistan through Pakistan in what has been called "the largest and costliest American covert operation since the Vietnam War."[56] The United States has not been alone among industrialized nations in engaging in this activity, exemplified by a West German firm sending the components for an entire ammunition production plant to arms-embargoed South Africa in the early 1980s, a British firm secretly supplying weapons and ammunition to Burma in defiance of an arms embargo in 1990, and even a Swedish company sending military explosives to Iran in the mid-1980s in defiance of Swedish export regulations.[57] The Third World is also joining the fray of covert selling at the global arms bazaar, shown by Libya's secret transfer of arms and explosives to the Irish Republican Army in 1985–1986 and Iran's clandestine shipments of weapons to the Bosnian Muslims in 1993.[58] Covert transnational flows of arms thus go both from governments to private groups and from private groups to governments, and while both kinds of transfers are worrisome they create different kinds of dangers.

SECURITY IMPLICATIONS

Perhaps more directly than any of the other flows in this study, clandestine arms transfers have a major security impact. The international arms distribution system tends to move firepower quickly to the most volatile areas of the world, increasing the likelihood that a spark of turmoil will ignite into a flame of violent war, that the conflict will last longer and will involve more casualties, and that stable long-term resolution of the tensions will be harder to attain. Despite the alarming security threats posed by transnational transfers of small arms, governments have been slow to focus on this issue, preferring instead to concentrate on major weapons systems. Recently, however, "thanks largely to the efforts of grassroots groups, the full costs of small arms proliferation are beginning to attract the attention of policy makers: the loss of life and property, the climate of fear and pervasive instability, the disruption of economic development, and the threat to democratic governance that result from the violence made possible by wide availability of small arms."[59] The concern about the covert international traffic in small arms has grown so substantially that in April 1998 the United States co-sponsored a United Nations resolution aimed at curbing the illicit firearms trade.

It has taken the major powers a considerable amount of time to see the issue of the transfer of small and light weapons as a sufficiently grave security threat as to warrant their concerted attention. In July 1998, 21 nations met in Oslo, Norway in the first effort of its kind to try to stop the spread of these widely used arms across national boundaries. But the United States, wary after the pressure from the land mines treaty which it still has not signed, wanted to proceed slowly and deal only with the illicit clandestine arms traffic (this position also received support from France, China, and Russia, some of whom would not even attend the conference); in contrast, Belgium, Canada, and Norway wanted to move faster and more comprehensively to reduce light weapons transactions.[60] The differences here appear to be sufficiently deep as to prove quite thorny to resolve.

Having deadly arms transferred across national boundaries usually creates more security concerns than if the same weapons were developed internally. It is generally accepted that reliance on one's own arms sacrifices capability, while reliance on arms transfers from abroad sacrifices control.[61] Weapons transfers appear to have a more direct impact than internal arms development on changing the influence or dependence relationship between an initiating and receiving state in a more volatile direction because these transactions serve not only to interconnect the two nations' military capabilities but also potentially to increase their anxiety about each other's foreign security policies. Moreover, "the weapons trade may often trigger higher threat perception in the eyes of neighboring or enemy states—due to the assumption of heightened military ties to external powers—than would internal arms development."[62]

In a parallel fashion, having a significant proportion of the global arms traffic be covert dramatically increases the security threat. To begin with, "arms transferred under such illicit or semi-illicit deals appear more likely to be used in battle than normal legal government-to-government transfers since pressure for them is more likely to stem from immediate war needs;" and thus these deals represent "a challenge to government policymaking because they generally occur without full official consideration or public debate and because they increase the chances and severity of further fighting."[63] Beyond ordinary soldiers fighting in the many ongoing low-level shooting conflicts, terrorist and drug traffickers seem to be the most security-challenging recipients of clandestine arms flows, with the black market in armaments appearing to be more important to drug cartels than to any other non-state actor.[64] With national governments the largest regular suppliers of weapons to the covert arms trade,[65] this activity undermines the credibility of arms control initiatives and, indeed, the moral authority of major power suppliers.[66] With the most eager national recipients being widely embargoed rogue states such as Iran and North Korea,[67] the potential seems quite high for security disruption and, more specifically, upset of the military balance in such volatile regions as the Middle East and East Asia.[68] In sum, the illegal global arms trade can increase the threat by expanding the number and power of disruptive actors in the international system, complicating intelligence on the military capabilities of potential adversaries, frustrating attempts to restrain the military escalation or geographical spread of conflicts, penetrating national military supply systems and impeding the readiness of national military forces, and damaging foreign relations between the parties supplying the arms and the enemies of the parties receiving the arms.[69]

In the previous bipolar era, major powers often viewed with some justification the spread of arms across national boundaries as an effective means of enhancing stability both within and across states. Whether the weapons were transmitted overtly or covertly, the careful channeling of coercive capabilities to allies to protect themselves against external foes and to regimes under siege internally to prevent collapse and the "falling domino" effect appeared to represent a prudent application of deterrence logic to maintain order. However, in today's anarchic post–Cold War global setting, using cross-national arms transactions as a fine-tuned instrument to maintain national and international stability seems doomed to failure from the outset.

In the end, the deadly transfer of clandestine arms across national boundaries appears to link directly to all three protection goals—biological survival, political authority, and socioeconomic cohesion. Given that such weapons are largely used not for peacekeeping, hunting, or recreational purposes, the link to violence against both people and property seems to be inescapable. While human death is certainly the most important concern here, the impact on environmental destruction should not be overlooked. Turning to political authority, the reality that insurgent groups play such a prominent role as recipients of the contraband arms traffic[70] demonstrates a clear threat to the survival of status quo political regimes. While arms do not cause revolutions, they certainly do empower the discontent. Finally, the spread of coercive "might makes right" instruments among the mass population certainly rips at the fabric of civil society, increasing the probability that disagreements will be settled outside of normal channels, internal strife will not be resolved peacefully, resented economic costs to the rest of society will escalate, and that fear and distrust will undermine existing social institutions.

Chapter 5

Illegal Migrant Flows

In the context of the global playground, illegal migrants represent the largely unwanted intruders that either actually engage in the mischief on the playground or are held responsible by others for any problems that emerge.[71] Because these undocumented aliens are not legitimate players on the playground, they have no rights, so they are often abused and mistreated by others without fear of notice or retribution. At the same time, however, these unsanctioned intruders often feel that they do not need to play by the rules of the playground, and they are often ignorant of what the rules actually are. What complicates the situation further is that often those who sneak into the confines of the playground may be aided, or even enticed and facilitated, by unruly players who themselves legitimately belong on the playground. Moreover, the playground monitors may turn a blind eye toward these intruders because they end up performing some unwanted menial tasks on the playground that the monitors find useful. The net effect of all this complexity is that effective playground management becomes a nightmare.

SCOPE OF THE PROBLEM

Illegal migration across national boundaries incorporates both those pushed out by horrendous conditions at home and those pulled in by attractive conditions abroad, with in all cases an express violation of the national immigration laws of receiving states. While many illegal aliens make and execute on their own the decision to move (often with some help from relatives and friends in both the country of origin and the country of destination), an increasing proportion of this undocumented migration ends up under the facilitating influence or control of transnational criminal organizations who find that smuggling human contraband across borders is a highly lucrative business.[72] The human contraband smuggled includes not only cheap menial labor but also prostitutes and criminals, with economic profit being the sole unifying thread. This smuggling appears to be a "low risk, high gain" proposition: porous global borders and high-volume international human traffic make detection difficult; and the penalties for human smuggling in the United States and Western Europe are relatively lenient compared to those for smuggling narcotics, with the penalties in the rest of the world for human smuggling even slighter.[73] Part of the explanation for the lenient penalties lies in the mixed feelings recipient societies have about unsanctioned aliens because "most unauthorized immigrants concentrate in jobs that have long been abandoned by the country's legal work force."[74]

The worldwide profits of international smugglers of illegal aliens are about $7 billion a year, with the price for a single individual to be transported often in the $30,000 range.[75] The total number of illegal migrants crossing national borders in 1996 was between 10 and 30 million compared to about 100 million legal global migrants that year.[76] About 10 to 15 percent of the immigrants in rich countries are unauthorized, and while most enter by illegal means a significant minority enters legally but fails to depart when their visas expire.[77] Some of these illegal migrants consider themselves—or are considered by some humanitarian groups—to be refugees fleeing from undesirable situations, as one out of every 130 persons in the world was displaced by war or persecution in 1995.[78]

RECENT HISTORY

Smuggling people across borders has, of course, a long and sordid history, as "until just a few centuries ago slavery and slave trading were legal and commonplace features of society and commerce throughout the world."[79] However, long after the world began to view the slave trade as both morally and legally unacceptable, illegal migration to the industrialized world has continued, with the numbers increasing significantly over the last decade:[80] in the United States, despite an official policy of penalizing employers for hiring illegal aliens, between 200,000 and 300,000 undocumented migrants flow across the border from Mexico each year; the number of illegal migrants to Western Europe has risen dramatically to approach 3 million, largely from Eastern Europe and Africa; and Japan now faces increased illegal migration from mainland China, the Philippines, and other parts of Southeast Asia. The Third World has experienced a similar pattern of increase in recent years, with growing illegal labor flows from Indonesia to Malaysia, from Bangladesh to India, from Nepal to Bhutan, from China to Hong Kong and Taiwan, and from many parts of Africa to Ivory Coast, South Africa, and Nigeria.[81]

The reasons for this increased illegal migration include the increased restrictions on legal migration by both developed and developing nations since the 1970s; the growth in global markets, stimulating the development of migration networks; the removal of obstacles to migration due to the breakdown of authoritarian regimes; and, most directly, the emergence of transnational criminal groups—"migration mafia"—that "extract fees from would-be migrants (sometimes turning illegal migrants into bonded laborers) to arrange their transportation and employment abroad."[82] The most basic motives of illegal migrants continue to include not only the desperate attempt to escape from poverty but also a "revolution of rising expectations" associated with improving economic conditions in their home states.[83] Despite the increased ability of people in one country to be aware of conditions in another, illegal migrants are still often victims of the optimistic misconception that their destinations have "streets paved with gold."

Brief comments on a few of the more prominent illegal migrant flows serve to illustrate the general patterns. Perhaps the most widely analyzed flow of illegal aliens are those moving from Mexico to the United States along their long-shared border, driven not only by poverty, unemployment, and income disparities but also by the web of social and family connections Mexicans have in the United States, the experience of Mexicans living in the United States, and the increasing interconnectedness of the Mexican and American economies.[84] Less widely noticed are the flows of about 100,000 illegal Chinese migrants into the United States each year, smuggled in by criminal groups for huge fees and then forced to work in menial jobs in vain attempts to repay their debt in circumstances that can only be described as "virtual slavery";[85] and the flows of illegal Cubans into the United States, recently restricted through a bilateral agreement but in the past purposefully stimulated by Fidel Castro and the Cuban government as a way of directing tens of thousands of "undesirables"—including criminals and mentally ill people—into the United States as part of what some describe as "demographic warfare."[86]

The rest of the industrialized world faces similar dilemmas concerning illegal migration: Germany recently faced mounting pressure to send back home 40,000 Vietnamese migrants who had settled in East Germany as guest workers in textile factories and light industry but who Germany classified as illegal aliens;[87] and Japan has been facing an internal debate about its over 280,000 illegal migrants that has moved beyond simply labor market issues to encompass potentially racist arguments about the need to preserve a homogeneous society.[88] In the Third World, Malaysia faces sizable illegal migration from neighboring areas, particularly from the Philippines, from which about 350,000 have fled from poverty and strife, and the result has been a significant increase in ethnic tensions;[89] and Costa Rica faces the problem that its large undocumented migrant population—estimated between 80,000 and 223,000 during the 1980s—ironically enjoys fewer restrictions than its officially recognized refugee population.[90] While the motives for this wide range of cases of illegal migration are largely economic, the difficulties engendered are often cultural in nature.

SECURITY IMPLICATIONS

The security implications deriving from illegal migration appear to be more indirect but perhaps more wide-ranging than those associated with clandestine arms transfers. The international climate has generally become a lot more openly hostile toward any approximation of open borders; long gone is the humanitarian sentiment reflected in Emma Lazarus' famous poem inviting in the "tired, poor, tempest-tossed huddled masses yearning to breathe free." The international community has made it clear for some time that it views the free movement of people across borders in a radically different—and more restrictive—way than the free movement of goods, capital, and services.[91] In contrast to receptivity toward cross-national flows of non-permanent tourists, "the specter of the long term mass transfer of desperate (and frequently undesired) humans across state boundaries associates with a uniquely acute sense of peacetime threat to sovereignty in the current international system."[92] Much of this sense of threat appears to originate at the grassroots level, as illegal migrants send bottom-up shock waves through affected societies, with national governments often bearing the brunt of widespread popular fears.

The general defense-related consequences of this flow of unsanctioned people across borders seems to be confrontation, avoidance, and discrimination:[93] confrontation involves expanding internal and external conflict within and between the home state and the host state of the migrants, with pressure to resolve or eliminate differences by force; avoidance entails growing public xenophobia within receiving states, with pressure to send illegal migrants home and close borders; and discrimination encompasses intensifying competition for goods and services within receiving states, with pressure to protect the advantages of the native population. The movement of illegal migrants highlights deep moral dilemmas that national government officials are loath to discuss among themselves or with the public. In overburdening domestic social service systems and raising the crime rate, illegal aliens often cause increasingly putative laws to go into effect in receiving societies aimed at all immigrants.[94] In the end, illegal migration can disrupt the relationship between state and society— "many citizens feel that their governments have lost control of their borders, and governments are in turn alarmed by the growing hostility of their citizens to the foreigners living and working in their midst."[95] While legal migration clearly can be quite beneficial to receiving states, this covert transnational flow has the potential to produce considerable social and economic instability.

Sensing increasing burdens, risks, and disruptions within receiving states often translates into attributing threat to the presence of illegal migrants. Amplified by the proximity of the distinctive needs and practices of these unauthorized newcomers, the citizenry may feel both scarcity and divisiveness within their societies and a loss of control over preservation of its traditional distinctive features. As a result, undocumented aliens may shoulder the brunt of the blame for any real or imagined domestic problems, including disease, crime, overpopulation, land degradation, or any form of downturn in the cherished comfortable lifestyles of the indigenous population. Then disgruntled citizens tend to turn their anger toward their own governments, claiming these regimes have not adequately protected their native rights and way of life.

It is indeed a sad commentary on the state of cross-cultural tolerance in modern society that illegal migrants appear to cause the greatest socioeconomic turmoil in receiving states when they differ racially and ethnically, or to a lesser extent linguistically or religiously, from the citizenry of the society which they enter. It is not just the so-called dispassionate issues of job loss and financial burdens that underlie the concerns about the unsanctioned newcomers, but rather a more emotional sense of dread that they will overwhelm, pollute, degrade, and ultimately destroy the dominant culture and genetic composition of the indigenous society. In multicultural receiving states like the United States, the notion of the "melting pot"—which made both documented and undocumented aliens a lot more palatable because of the belief that they would eventually accept and assimilate into the prevailing belief system—has been replaced by a separatist image of "tribalism" and "ethnic enclaves" that appears considerably more threatening to the existing citizenry. In largely monoethnic receiving states (such as Japan), the high value placed on ethnic homogeneity makes pervasive perceived threat particularly likely when culturally dissimilar migrants enter their societies.[96]

While some might argue that these concerns do not really pose major threats to national security, and instead simply constitute minor issues relevant to the smooth functioning of domestic society, this dismissive attitude is becoming much more of a minority position in today's fearful global environment. It is far more common now to see references to the dangers posed by illegal migrant flows (in a manner similar to Machiavelli) as comparable to that posed by invading armies.[97] In Western Europe, in particular, illegal migrants and refugees appear to trigger a dominant nativist fear by both governments and citizens, bandied about on more than one occasion by politicians to inflame debate about more restrictive immigration laws: this fear revolves around the specter of hordes of unsanctioned aliens from the Third World pouring into these advanced industrialized nations to escape the utter misery experienced in the deprived places from which these desperate travelers flee. Even in the United States, the depth of the widespread terror of being overwhelmed from abroad is perhaps best illustrated by President Clinton's announcement in September 1994 that the United States intended to invade Haiti unless its military regime relinquished power, with his statement being a direct response to the overwhelming domestic outrage about the flood of illegal migrants (and refugees) from Haiti to the United States fleeing from both poverty and political oppression.

Although most of the concern about the security implications of illegal migration focuses on the threat to receiving states, sending states also suffer. Buoyed by messages from friends and relatives who have managed successfully to make an illegal crossing into another country, the citizenry of sending states may become simultaneously attracted by external opportunities in receiving states and frustrated and intolerant of internal conditions within their own countries. A common result is that sending state governments become the targets of accusations of incompetence, corruption, or even secret encouragement of the illegal migration, undermining both the legitimacy and stability of the regimes. The dangers embedded in these accusations may only worsen if disgruntled illegal migrants are detected by receiving states and forced to return home. A representative example of sending state troubles stimulated by illegal out-migration occurred in August 1994, when several thousand illegal Cuban migrants left their homeland for the Florida coast; the tensions prompted the United States to negotiate an agreement with Cuba allowing a certain number of legal Cuban migrants annually on the condition that the Cuban government would forcibly prevent unauthorized people from leaving in the future,[98] a consequence that would almost certainly place major stress on that regime.

Illegal migration across national boundaries thus most directly affects the security protection goal of socioeconomic cohesion within recipient societies. There appears to be no direct impact here either on biological survival, as illegal migrants do not automatically appear more prone to violence than citizens, or on political authority, as these unsanctioned aliens do not seem more likely than citizens to endeavor to overthrow an existing government. But these undocumented aliens do often inadvertently end up (at least in the short-term) turning members of one's own society against each other, increasing the economic costs citizens have to pay for these unsanctioned residents' education and health care, and causing troublesome questions to be raised about the basic values of a nation and its people. Illegal migrants quite frequently suffer hardship and deprivation on their way to their new home, and in today's restrictive world it seems far less likely that they would attain even a significant piece of their dreams of economic well-being; as a result, the socioeconomic cohesion among the unsanctioned migrants themselves, both broadly and within individual families, is also really put to the test.

Chapter 6

Illicit Drug Flows

The deadly transfer of illicit drugs serves two very different purposes on the global playground. First, this activity allows those cynical and disillusioned members of the playground to find a means of seemingly pleasurable escape from confronting the harsh realities that surround them. Second, drugrunning permits the unruly players on the playground to use an extremely profitable way to incapacitate a substantial proportion of the playground community, simultaneously neutralizing any potential opponents and dragging in recipients of the narcotics into a complex cornucopia of crime. Because a prevailing view of these unsanctioned substances is that they cause severe physical harm to individuals who use them but generate little direct damage to the society as a whole, it is quite common for playground monitors to turn a blind eye to this activity, implicitly figuring that those sufficiently short-sighted not to realize the dangers involved deserve whatever negative consequences they suffer. Indeed, for these reasons the playgrounds in parks in major cities have become perhaps the prime location for buying and selling illicit drugs.

SCOPE OF THE PROBLEM

The illicit transfer of psychoactive drugs across national bound-aries involves both mild narcotics such as marijuana (cannabis) and severe ones such as heroin (opium) and cocaine.[99] Within most societies considerable debate exists about how different these prohibited substances are from nicotine in cigarettes, alcohol in liquor, and even caffeine in coffee and tea: all provide a physical release that many people find to be pleasurable, and all are dan-gerous or even lethal when taken in very high concentrations or over a very long period of time. For this reason, the possibility of legalization of the transnational flow of these substances comes up with a frequency and intensity unmatched by the other deadly transfers.

The global drug trade nets between $420 billion and $1 trillion a year, making it about three-fifths the size of the federal budget of the United States and making illicit drugs the single best-selling product in the world.[100] The United Nations Drug Control Pro-gramme conservatively estimated in 1996 the annual turnover in the global illicit drug trade to be $500 billion.[101] The United States is the largest consumer, with 30 million American users spending per year about $28 billion on cocaine, $68 billion on marijuana, and $10 to $12 billion on heroin.[102] The impact of these illicit nar-cotics on American life is painfully clear, with 14,000 drug-related deaths each year, a soaring prison population, and indirect costs estimated at $67 billion a year.[103] Most states of the world play a part in the global market for prohibited drugs, "a market almost as large as those for the major permitted drugs—nicotine and al-cohol."[104] A 1991 report of the United Nations International Nar-cotics Control Board confirmed that "the use, cultivation, and smuggling of drugs" and the "laundering of proceeds" are rap-idly "spreading around the planet in the last decade of the 20th century."[105]

The major international drug money laundering sites include countries as diverse as the Cayman Islands, Colombia, Germany, Hong Kong, Italy, Mexico, the Netherlands, Nigeria, Panama, Sin-gapore, Switzerland, Thailand, the United Kingdom, the United States, and Venezuela.[106] The monetary costs of the global drug operation are staggering but of course more than offset by the monetary benefits: a leading drug baron boasted that he authorized payments of $1 million a day to keep himself out of jail, and a Colombian cocaine cartel is reputed to pay between 17 and 20 percent for money laundering services that transfer drug profits into cash-intensive travel agencies, exchange houses, casinos, international trading firms, and building construction operations.[107] However, not just transnational criminal groups but also rogue states are horning in on the international drug action, as at various times the governments of Bolivia, Nicaragua, Panama, Cuba, Bulgaria, Syria, and Serbia have been accused of a "willing dip into the commerce of heroin, opium, and cocaine."[108]

A common explanation for this lucrative transnational business is inadequate success within source states in producing traditional agricultural goods—"because farmers in countries like Bolivia, Peru, and Colombia have great difficulty securing access to markets for their food crops or selling them at an adequate price . . . they often have little choice but to grow coca and other illegal drugs."[109] Due to the huge number of coca farmers, exporters, and smugglers, the supply of cocaine is difficult to eliminate, and the rewards from selling it are great because the price rises roughly 200 times between the coca farm and the street.[110] Drug traders generally view globalization as their "greatest growth opportunity,"[111] and given the reluctance of either drug-consuming or drug-producing nations to take direct responsibility for the problem, these traders feel with considerable justification that they can consistently evade local authorities.[112]

RECENT HISTORY

Looking at the history of international drug trafficking, one quickly discovers that "the desire of individuals to alter their state of consciousness is one of the few constants of civilized human history," with a variety of psychoactive substances used for thousands of years for medicinal, ritual, and recreational purposes, and that this use was not globally censured until the twentieth century.[113] One recent development that has complicated the management of transnational drug flows has been the growth in the production of "designer drugs" and synthetic narcotics, allowing their creators to enjoy a brief "window of legality" before the regulatory system catches up to them.[114] The global "war on drugs" began in the United States in 1986 when President Reagan identified illicit drug traffic as a national security threat and authorized the Defense Department to engage in anti-drug operations, leading to interdiction expenditures that grew from $400 million in 1987 to $1.2 billion in 1991;[115] but widespread consensus exists that this effort has largely failed to make a dent in the illicit drug trade.[116]

Examining the case of the world's best-known drug exporter—Colombia, the most important source of cocaine and marijuana transported to North America—helps to illustrate the general nature of this flow. Colombian drug dealers have created elaborate transnational trade networks and, when challenged, have engaged in assassination, bribery of international officials, and even full-scale military assaults.[117] When the Cuban mafia fled to the United States in the early 1960s in the wake of Castro's ascendancy, they used Colombia as the primary source of their drugs. Colombia's gradual emergence as Latin America's preeminent drug supplier was due to its geopolitical position, its vast central forests that effectively hide secret processing laboratories and airstrips facilitating the traffic, the strong entrepreneurial skills of the Colombian people, and the willingness of the Colombian community in the United States to function as a distributor network.[118] A "drug-insurgency nexus" has appeared to develop in which leftist guerrillas work hand in hand with drug dealers to help undermine the U.S. government through the influx of illicit narcotics, thereby weakening the "dependent-capitalist state" in Colombia and accelerating the pace of revolutionary change there.[119] Today Colombia is the leading refiner and distributor of cocaine, with its annual production of 80 metric tons accounting for three-quarters of the global supply, and it has recently (1) vertically integrated by branching out into cultivation of the coca plant and (2) diversified into more extensive cultivation, production, and distribution of marijuana and heroin.[120]

Of course, the recent intensification of the global drug trafficking problem is confined neither to Colombia nor to cocaine: the world's first independent mafia state emerged in 1993, as a powerful mafia family living in Sicily and Venezuela bought the sovereign Caribbean island of Aruba using a fortune amassed through the North American heroin trade.[121] And when it comes to heroin, Burma cultivates the majority of the opium that is turned into heroin for a booming Asian drug market.[122] No region of the world can proudly state that it is untouched by narcotics trafficking. These examples hint at the incredible sophistication of modern drugrunners, comparable in many ways to the most efficient multinational corporations.

SECURITY IMPLICATIONS

The security implications of the covert transnational flow of illicit drugs appear to involve the gradual decay from within of nation-states. On the social level, this trafficking associates in consuming states with a rapid rise in drug-related violent crimes in inner cities and escalating health care problems, including the accelerated spread of AIDS via drug users.[123] The spread of illicit drugs links directly to the deadly transfer of clandestine arms, hazardous materials, and infectious diseases. While the decay involved is often less immediately visible than that linked to the other transfers, it seems just as damaging.

On the political-military level, the American promotion of the use of military force to fight drug traffickers in some states has the potential to lead to an undue strengthening of this coercive element within the fragile democracies in drug-producing states.[124] While attempting to promote political stability, the war on drugs can clearly have an unintended backfire effect here in which the elements of a country strengthened to combat drugrunners end up short-circuiting the proper functioning of democracy. Without popular support and understanding of these anti-drug initiatives, the result can easily turn into political and social turmoil.

On the economic level, a primary response to several major source countries—including Burma and Colombia—has been to "decertify" them for not cooperating in the war on drugs, and as a result these states do not qualify for credit from the Export-Import Bank or the Overseas Private Investment Corporation.[125] However, the strength of the black market and transshipment options makes these gestures somewhat hollow. Moreover, the profits generated from transnational drug sales can easily overshadow these financial losses.

Finally, drug-related corruption (termed "narco-corruption") is spreading across regimes in both producing and consuming societies, and in the process is posing a major global security threat.

With both the police and key government officials directly caught in the lucrative drug web, corrupted individuals tend to lose their sense of dignity and integrity, and corrupted governments tend to lose whatever sense of confidence and legitimacy they possess in the eyes of their citizenry and fellow nations.[126] A 1993 survey of anti-drug enforcement bodies (including the police, customs officials, and the judiciary) tainted by drug money shows that corruption exists at the most senior levels in Afghanistan, Armenia, Argentina, Azerbaijan, Bolivia, Colombia, the Dominican Republic, Ecuador, Guatemala, Honduras, India, Iran, Italy, Kenya, Laos, Mexico, Morocco, Nicaragua, Niger, Nigeria, Pakistan, Panama, Paraguay, Peru, the Philippines, Romania, Senegal, Spain, Suriname, Syria, Tajikistan, Thailand, Turkey, Venezuela, and Zambia.[127] More than any of the other ominous transnational flows, the level of influence illicit drug sales provide for transnational criminal organizations over the governments of key source countries are a major source of instability.

One of the major reasons illicit drugs still pose a significant security threat is that effective international collaboration is so difficult on this issue. International conferences attempting to deal with this issue have been specifically hampered by "a combination of political rivalries, jealously guarded national legal systems, official corruption and sheer incompetence."[128] Even if such meetings proved fruitful, their actions appear likely to be "preempted" by transnational criminal organizations controlling the illicit drugs traffic; the members of these syndicates are "cosmopolitan businessmen, well-educated, well-spoken, who know how to move among politicians and officials and transfer money from Wall Street to London to Paris and beyond . . . they are privileged people, with plenty of opportunities . . . just more than usually greedy as businessmen and so tempted to take the criminal route."[129]

Another major reason this drug-related security threat persists is the insistence of policy makers in industrialized nations on attacking only the supply end of the problem. The supply-side approach appears deficient because "the profitability of the current system is so great that even dramatically improved success in supply-side enforcement (interdiction of production and distribution) will only marginally offset the incentive for generating new sources."[130] As a result, in 1992 the Central Intelligence

Agency concluded that these supply-side efforts to reduce the flow of illicit drugs have largely failed.[131]

This reluctance to attack both the demand for and the supply of illicit drugs relates to another explanation of the persistence of the drug trafficking problem—the steadfast refusal of anyone to be accountable for the problem. Drug-consuming and drug-producing nations continually engage in futile finger pointing at each other, with each blaming the other for the pernicious consequences of these shady transactions.[132] A classic example here is the relationship between the United States and Mexico: on the drug issue "each blames the other for its woes" and "each largely ignores its own flaws"; "Americans are preoccupied with addiction and crime, Mexicans with violence and corruption, yet the problems of one are rapidly becoming a menace in the other."[133] As long as this irresponsible attitude toward illicit drug transfers persists, the drug trade will flourish.

Part of the underlying security problem here is that the threats posed by the illicit traffic in drugs to sending states and receiving states are really quite different. Sending states generally appear to be more concerned with issues of government corruption, distortions in the domestic economy through misallocation of agricultural land, and a tarnished international image that leads to the possibility of international sanctions taken against them. Receiving states, on the other hand, generally seem more concerned with the distraction and degeneration of their citizens who become hooked on drugs and the consequent empowerment of organized crime which controls the distribution of the illicit substances within their boundaries. So it is not only the irrational finger pointing but also the quite rational differences in security impacts that impede collective problem solving here.

Finally, the global drug trafficking problem continues because national governments are distracted by other sources of ongoing problems. Due to the aforementioned complicity of many of these governments in the drug trade—the division of public opinion on the issue, the finger pointing among states, and states' underlying sluggishness in recognizing the security threat it poses—they often look for other explanations of turmoil. Afghanistan provides a vivid example here, as "the insidious influence of the drugs trade has spread through all layers of society" at a time "when violent turmoil caused by other forces—such as the collapse of the Soviet empire coinciding with the revival of Islamic fundamentalism—has occupied official attention elsewhere."[134] In situations like this one it is certainly easy to understand how the deadly transfer of drugs (in this case, opium) might not be seen as significant enough even to make a blip on the international radar screen.

While the primary security protection goal affected by the deadly transfer of illicit drugs across national boundaries is socioeconomic cohesion, there is an important impact on biological survival and political authority as well. More subtly than any other ominous transnational flow discussed in this study, narcotics transactions eat away at the core of what makes a civil community function properly, drastically skewing the flow of revenues, enhancing the power of organized crime, and hooking individuals into a life of eternal craving devoid of any stable, long-term fulfillment. The issue of biological survival, largely confined to those who ingest the drugs, involves the human death caused by drug overdoses and contaminated drugs and needles. As to political authority, the severity of the predicament in parts of Latin America shows that it is not inconceivable for an entire national government (and its security policies) to be held hostage to the rich and heavily armed criminal organizations controlling the drug traffic.

Chapter 7

Hazardous Materials Flows

On the global playground, the deadly transfer of unsanctioned hazardous materials reflects a thoughtless dumping of one's toxic garbage without any concern for the impact on the lives of other people living near the dumping areas or on the sustainability of the local environment. Just as many individuals discard their refuse in school and park playgrounds as a means of avoiding both pickup fees and the dangers of keeping the waste close to them, so nations and companies on the international level secretly transfer hazardous materials out of their countries as a means of avoiding penalties and livability consequences within their own societies. The "not-in-my-backyard" mentality pervades the global playground—if it is possible to "solve" a problem by simply moving it away from your geographical zone of concern, who cares about anyone else? Given that the hazardous materials ultimately land usually not within someone's private property but rather within "common-pool" public areas, it is easy to rationalize this movement (like so many of the other deadly transfers) as a perfectly innocuous activity.

SCOPE OF THE PROBLEM

Of all the ominous flows considered in this study, the movement of unsanctioned hazardous materials across national boundaries has received by far the least attention.[135] Part of the problem here is the paucity of knowledge about this transnational flow, with little reliable data even on open official interstate hazardous material transfers. Another explanation for the ignorance about this issue and the inattention it receives is that it is often falsely classified as a strictly environmental problem rather than as a security concern.

Hazardous materials include both conventional toxic wastes and nuclear materials, especially weapons-grade plutonium and uranium. A major contributor to the inattention and ignorance has been the ongoing controversy about how to define hazardous materials, which in theory could mean virtually any substance if stored or transported improperly in sufficient volume: perhaps the most widely accepted notion encompasses any material that poses a substantial threat to human health or the environment when managed improperly, including a variety of toxic, ignitable, corrosive, or dangerously reactive substances such as acids, cyanides, pesticides, herbicides, solvents, obsolete explosives, nerve gas, radioactive material, sewage sludge, PCBs and dioxins, fly ash from power plants, infectious waste from hospitals and research laboratories, and compounds of lead, mercury, arsenic, cadmium, and zinc.[136] While the scope of this problem area is obviously difficult to specify exactly, the best guess is that the world produces about 338 million tons of hazardous waste annually; global trade in this waste is a multibillion dollar industry, with the American import and export of precious metals waste alone exceeding $1 billion a year.[137] The exact proportion of these transactions that are unsanctioned is hard to detect, in part because governments are continually claiming that they had no knowledge or approval of transfers that end up being globally condemned for harmful effects.

RECENT HISTORY

A historical perspective indicates that since World War II, "the amount of toxic byproducts created by the manufacturers of pharmaceuticals, petroleum, nuclear devices, pesticides, chemicals and other allied products has increased almost exponentially," leading to a rise globally in the transboundary movement of hazardous waste.[138] While much of this trade occurs between advanced industrialized nations with highly developed regulatory regimes ensuring the environmentally sound management of the hazardous materials, a significant proportion flows from developed states to developing countries that lack the proper means of disposal.[139] The motives for this North-South flow of waste include not only the "not-in-my-backyard" mentality of the industrialized states but also a widespread belief that "the economic logic behind dumping a load of toxic waste in the lowest wage country is impeccable" because the costs and concern surrounding environmental protection are lowest there.[140]

On May 5, 1992, The Basel Convention on the Transboundary Movement of Hazardous Wastes and Their Disposal went into effect, requiring signatories to adhere to a notice-and-consent procedure and to take into account whether recipients will handle waste in an environmentally sound manner, but this has by no means resolved the international concerns or the negative impact of these dangerous transactions. Even with the agreement in September 1995 by over 100 countries to amend the Basel Convention to ban the export of hazardous waste from the rich nations to the poor ones, this legislation may have served largely to push these transactions under the table. During the recent Fourth Conference of the Parties to the Basel Convention, held in Malaysia in February 1998, there was progress on the definition of hazardous wastes, but countries still differed markedly in their positions on international exchange of these substances.

Turning directly to the unsanctioned transnational flows of hazardous materials, the current predicament appears particularly foreboding. Strong incentives now exist to engage in surreptitious transfer of hazardous materials in order to avoid both paying relevant taxes and abiding by cost-increasing government regulations designed to minimize environmental damage.[141] Although no means are available to estimate the magnitude of these covert flows, there is every reason to believe that these transactions— including nuclear smuggling—are rising because "the large profits to be made from their disposal encourage illegal trafficking"; and a United Nations study concludes that the "foremost characteristic of illegal traffic in toxic and dangerous products is the dominant movement of these substances from the industrial to the developing world."[142] It seems no coincidence that the most common direction of the flow of unsanctioned hazardous materials is also politically the most volatile.

Some truly noteworthy incidents of unsanctioned hazardous materials transfers have occurred in recent years. Between August 1987 and May 1988, in a deal arranged by an Italian trader with a Nigerian national, five ships transported over 8,000 drums containing 3,800 tons of hazardous wastes (some of which contained PCBs, some of the world's most toxic pollutants) from various European countries and the United States to Koko, Nigeria; when residents near the dirt lot where the waste was dumped fell seriously ill and Nigerian officials found falsely labeled leaky drums full of the waste, the Italian government eventually had to send two ships to pick up the waste and to return it to Italy and repackage it for disposal.[143] In spring 1987 the Mexican navy had to prevent forcibly the unsanctioned dumping by an American garbage barge of over 3,000 tons of hazardous wastes in Mexico; a common reaction to the incident was that it exemplified the "scorn" some in the United States felt toward Mexico, viewing it as their "outhouse."[144] In June 1996, 640 tons of urban Californian trash somehow ended up in a suburb of Beijing, China: faced with a stinking pile of refuse containing sewage, used syringes, and a decomposing dog, the *China Daily* newspaper stated "if the U.S. government is concerned about human rights, it should . . . stop the dirty business."[145]

Looking specifically at nuclear materials, the prime example of transnational smuggling revolves around Russia. In addition to thousands of nuclear warheads being dismantled in that country in accordance with arms reduction treaties, there are about 1,500 tons of plutonium and highly enriched uranium stored in hundreds of poorly secured sites across the country: since the fall of the communist regime, there have been more than 800 attempts to smuggle illegally nuclear materials out of Russia and the former Soviet Republics, areas characterized by the pervasiveness of criminal influence and political instability, including (1) beryllium (used for high-grade nuclear weaponry) intercepted in Lithuania on its way to a buyer in Switzerland (probably representing North Korea) and (2) plutonium intercepted in Munich (very possibly on its way to Pakistan).[146] The disintegration of the Soviet Union has made access to weapons-grade materials so much easier than in the past that a Russian military prosecutor commented recently that "potatoes were guarded better" than weapons-usable nuclear fuel.[147] These cases suggest that global vigilance about unsanctioned hazardous materials transfers is even lower than that pertaining to clandestine arms, illegal migrants, or illicit drugs.

SECURITY IMPLICATIONS

Onlookers generally have more difficulty seeing the security impact of unsanctioned hazardous materials transfers compared with the other flows considered in this study. Illegal trafficking in hazardous materials is significantly more dangerous than legal trafficking "since the latter is at least governed by a regulatory regime that aspires to environmentally sound management."[148] It is not surprising that "it is the poor, the young, and the working class who suffer most" within states from hazardous waste,[149] just as it is the less developed countries who seem to suffer most from it on the international level. With the United Nations' Basel Convention widely considered to be "toothless,"[150] the political controversies along with the health and environmental hazards are continuing unabated.

Yet the impact of the unsanctioned hazardous materials trade on the stability of the relationship between the industrialized world and the Third World is a bit muddled. Several Third World countries, mostly in Africa, have labeled the secret dumping of toxic materials abroad as a form of "toxic terrorism" undertaken by Western "merchants of death."[151] However, when the industrialized world began seriously considering a formal ban on this flow in 1994, many Third World businesses complained that the move "represented a conspiracy by the developed world against them" because the ban included the transport of hazardous scrap materials which they have been using to recycle to produce aluminum, zinc, steel, and paper.[152]

India's participation in the international waste trade exemplifies the security complexities surrounding receiving state attitudes on hazardous waste flows from the industrialized world to the Third World. At the First Conference of Parties to the Basel Convention in Uruguay in November 1992, the head of the Indian delegation pleaded with industrialized nations to stop exporting hazardous waste, arguing "you industrialized countries have been asking us to do many things for the global good—to stop cutting down our forests, to stop using your CFCs . . . now we are asking you to do something for the global good: keep your own waste."[153] But later, in the months leading up to the Third Basel Conference of Parties in September 1995, "opponents of the ban, including industrialized governments and waste trading industries, lobbied Third World governments to back out of the ban at the upcoming meeting"; as a result, just weeks before the meeting, the Indian government (lobbied specifically by the United States and Australia) announced that it was reconsidering the ban and that it might continue to allow hazardous waste imports for recycling into India.[154] Indian officials pointed with pride at their Bhopal-based Bharat Zinc factory, which imports and processes hazardous materials to reclaim zinc, as a model recycling facility; but Greenpeace's International Toxic Trade Campaign revealed that the factory posed such significant health and safety hazards to its workers that the Indian Supreme Court stepped in and considered a petition to take action against the factory.[155] Greenpeace contends that "we in the West have conveniently moved the dirty part of the recycling process to Asia" and that "every Indian port is a floodgate . . . the world's waste traders know it . . . India is receiving the effluent of the affluent."[156] Clearly the lust for profits has taken priority over moral or environmental concerns for parties to these deadly transfers from both industrialized and developing nations.

In contrast, Germany's participation in international hazardous waste transactions typifies the security controversies swirling around sending state attitudes toward this North-South flow. Dubbed "the world champion waste exporter," Germany exported more than 600,000 tons of hazardous waste to ten countries in 1993.[157] Possessing a combination of "some of the world's best waste management regulations and some of the world's worst waste export laws," the economic incentives to send toxic refuse abroad have spawned a series of embarrassing international incidents: in November 1994, after much pressure from Greenpeace and exposure in the media, Germany took back 465 tons of repackaged waste pesticides it had sent to Albania in 1991–1992 under the false labeling of "humanitarian aid"; in 1993 Germany took back 450 tons of old pesticides in leaky drums it had shipped to Romania; and between 1990 and 1995 large quantities of German toxic waste have turned up in Poland, Estonia, Egypt, and the Black Sea, along with reported attempts to export incinerator slag, contaminated oil, and sewage sludge to Russia.[158] An official in the German government's environmental ministry claims that "many of the highly publicized incidents of recent years were illegal," and a senior German waste industry executive concurs by admitting "of course we cannot say that we are all angels and I am sure that we have people who are trying to make their fortunes at the margins."[159]

The most clear-cut security link is with the illegal smuggling of nuclear materials. Some have argued that "nuclear leakage"—the global spread of nuclear weapons or weapons-usable material—"constitutes the most serious direct threat to vital U.S. interests today and for the foreseeable future";[160] and the director of the Central Intelligence Agency recently characterized this flow as "a major national security threat," particularly if the primary recipients—as some believe—are transnational terrorist groups rather than transnational criminal organizations.[161] One of the major concerns here is that "the smuggling of nuclear materials may enable some country or crime group to independently produce a nuclear weapon, therefore raising the potential for nuclear blackmail."[162] For most countries, "the mere possibility of a black market in weapons-grade material is terrifying"; they fear that "instability would spread like a chain reaction" as "countries newly unsure about their neighbors' capabilities would find themselves ever more tempted to try to get a bomb themselves"; and they believe that "terrorist groups, kept from the nuclear game by their lack of industrial infrastructure, would become players" and "nuclear blackmailers could make a mint."[163] While the actual amount of nuclear materials that has been smuggled across national borders is miniscule compared to that of hazardous waste, alarm bells ring much louder for national governments.

Regardless of whether one is dealing with unsanctioned transfers of conventional waste or of nuclear materials, the sending and receiving societies have substantially different security concerns. Sending societies want to find a secure means of disposing of their hazardous materials outside of their boundaries, while receiving societies need to find means of disposing these materials within their borders that will not endanger human health or environmental sustainability. With both sets of states hoping to make economic gains as a result of these transactions, the possibility of successful collaboration seems remote.

The unsanctioned transfer of hazardous materials across national boundaries has its most direct impact on the security protection goal of biological survival. All over the world humans have fallen ill, experienced reproductive problems, or died because hazardous materials have been secretly dumped or stored near where they live. In some cases the perpetrators have been aware of the dangers and the probable consequences on human life, and in other cases the initiators have been blissfully ignorant; but the toll of human suffering is oblivious to this distinction. The physical environment has also taken a major hit here, with the often irreversible disruption in the health, diversity, and sustainability of natural ecosystems usually ending up indirectly endangering human life. The covert cross-boundary movement of conventional waste does not generally endanger the protection goal of political authority, as the toxic refuse is dumped far from government headquarters; but the dispersion of lethal nuclear materials placed in the wrong hands clearly could be used as an instrument to help to overthrow governments. Neither conventional waste nor nuclear materials in themselves appear to be a major element in disrupting the protection goal of socioeconomic cohesion.

Chapter 8

Infectious Disease Flows

Characterized by fast movement, crowding, close contact, and little supervision, the global playground is the ideal environment for the contagious spread of problems from player to player. In school playgrounds, for example, this is where highly transmittable medical problems such as pinkeye, lice, and fifth disease (a contagious children's skin rash) move in a seemingly unstoppable fashion from student to student. This spread of infectious diseases is clearly not the fault of the playground monitors, as even the most vigilant of them would not be able to spot the transmission of what is functionally invisible and has a sizable incubation period. Moreover, the players carrying dangerous parasites cannot be held accountable for the outbreak, for they themselves may be unaware of the dangers at the time. In a highly mobile and interdependent setting, it seems unreasonable to expect anyone to be able to insulate themselves completely from exposure to germs of all kinds. Of course, the most unruly players may consider intentionally transmitting infectious diseases in this environment, but even this premeditated activity would be hard to track in a an inherently anarchic setting. When a contagious epidemic does break out, regardless of whether its initiation was intentional or unintentional, panic appears to be the most likely outcome, as frightened members discover to their horror that there is no secure means to protect themselves.

SCOPE OF THE PROBLEM

This deadly transfer has received the most startling increase in attention in recent years, reflecting an almost paranoid obsession not only with the largely unintended spread of lethal diseases across national borders but also with the intentional international transmission of toxic biological agents (often called "bioterrorism") designed to destroy life in the target area. It is, of course, a given that infectious parasitic disease "plays a pervasive role in all life"[164] and in the security of nations, but in recent years the resurgence of epidemics and the specter of involvement of unruly players in this arena has in many ways recast the whole set of issues here. Epidemiologists and public health specialists have become more concerned with broad security concerns, and foreign policy specialists have been forced to try to learn more about microbes. For example, President Clinton's 1998 commencement address at the United States Naval Academy specifically emphasized that "as we approach the 21st century, our foes have extended the fields of battle . . . from the world's vast bodies of water to the complex workings of our own human body," as "terrorists, criminals, and hostile regimes could invade and paralyze" vital systems threatening the health of the nation.[165]

Reliable data on the scope and consequences of international flows of infectious diseases are hard to come by. The reasons for this include not only the usual difficulties in obtaining global information on issues that involve the mass public, but also an informal "gag rule" applying penalties to health care providers who report outbreaks, as governments and local elites fear that such reports will negatively affect foreign tourism and investment.[166] However, it is clear that the scope of the predicament is huge, as in 1995 more than 17 million people died globally from infectious parasitic diseases, accounting for more than one-quarter of all deaths.[167] Over 99 percent of the deaths from infectious diseases occur in developing countries, causing 42 percent of all deaths (16.3 million people) there.[168] Among the most highly publicized of the lethal worldwide infectious diseases are HIV and AIDS, with 8,823,000 global cases in 1990; tuberculosis, with 12,739,000 global cases in 1990; and diarrhea diseases, with 71,918,000 global cases in 1990.[169]

Within advanced industrialized societies, where infectious diseases are less of a problem, responsible for only 1.2 percent of deaths (135,000 people),[170] this deadly transfer is still a major concern. Using the United States—one of the healthiest nations in the world—to illustrate the problem, a White House interagency working group recently reported that since 1973 at least 29 previously unknown diseases appeared and 20 well-known ones have reappeared, often in deadlier forms.[171] Death rates in the United States from infectious parasitic diseases rose by 58 percent between 1980 and 1992, responsible in some way for 375,000 deaths—or 17 percent of all deaths—that last year.[172] As to biological agents subject to intentional transmission by those seeking to disrupt the system, the leading candidates are anthrax, brucellosis, the Ebola virus, the plague, tularemia, smallpox, the botulinum toxin, and ricin.[173] Although these biological agents have not caused nearly as many deaths as the leading infectious parasitic diseases mentioned earlier, they are "the most lethal substances known to mankind."[174] The potential danger here is perhaps best illustrated by the result of a well-known 1993 calculation by the United States Office of Technology Assessment revealing that "a single airplane delivering 100 kilograms (220 pounds) of anthrax spores over the District of Columbia could cause between 1 million and 3 million fatalities."[175]

RECENT HISTORY

While major epidemics have flowed across borders and ravaged human societies for centuries, during the twentieth century medical science injected a major note of optimism. Specifically, the public health establishment hoped that a "military-style campaign to obliterate viral, bacterial, and parasitic enemies" could end up "leaving the age of infectious disease permanently behind."[176] Unfortunately, this "grandiose optimism" relied on two faulty assumptions—that microbes were biologically static and that diseases could be quarantined geographically.[177] Thus in the early 1980s both the medical establishment and the general public were shocked to discover that the microbial adaptation was outstrip-

ping the ability of the scientific community to come up with remedial treatments, and the outbreak of the AIDS epidemic left
both groups convinced that their earlier optimistic visions were
grossly premature.[178] When old diseases resurfaced they often appeared in more drug-resistant forms, exemplified both by the well-
known resurgence of tuberculosis and by the less known new
form of cholera that has killed thousands of people in Africa and
Asia since 1995.[179] With the biological agents, where intentional
human intervention has played a much more prominent role, their
natural adaptive abilities could be accelerated by those intent on
disruption in such a way that they circumvent available vaccines
and antibiotics.[180] In recent years the accessibility of lethal biological agents has dramatically increased, as "bubonic plague bacte-
ria, deadly viruses, and toxins can either be obtained directly from
mail-order catalogues or stolen from laboratories and hospitals."[181] Recent advances in genetic engineering have permitted
new biological agents not only to be intentionally discovered and
stockpiled but also to be artificially created and synthesized (parallel in many ways to the development of artificial designer drugs
to meet the demand for illicit narcotics), reducing even further
defensive abilities to prepare for them in advance.

The explanation for the growing dangers associated with this
deadly transfer is quite multifaceted. The root causes include the
gradual breakdown of public health systems in many countries;
increasing urbanization and population density; development of
remote rain forest and savanna areas that expose human to dangerous microbes, such as the Ebola and Hantaan viruses, that previously only affected plants and animals; accelerating global
climate change that expands the habitats of mosquitoes and
disease-carrying pests; the spread of illicit drug use (discussed in
Chapter 6); and the migration explosion within and across countries, involving travel for business, recreation, and permanent re-
location that spread infectious parasitic diseases around the world
in a matter of hours.[182] An open, interdependent, expanding
global human population clearly presents a most vulnerable target
for this ominous transnational flow.

The major cases of international transmission of infectious parasitic diseases and lethal biological agents have received overwhelming publicity. Most notorious, of course, is the AIDS

epidemic, which the World Health Organization estimates "has infected a cumulative total of 30 million people and has become endemic to every country of the world."[183] While the HIV virus that causes AIDS is over a century old, a combination of forces in the late 1970s and early 1980s turned an obscure organism into a global plague:[184] increasing African urbanization, American and European intravenous drug use and homosexual activity in public bathrooms, the use of rape as a tool of ethnic cleansing in the 1977–1979 Uganda-Tanzania war, and the growth of international exports of contaminated American blood products. Because AIDS tends to kill young and middle-aged people, it can have a huge impact on a national population's life expectancy and growth, as has particularly been the case in several sub-Saharan African countries.[185] The direct and indirect worldwide costs of the disease are likely to exceed $500 billion by the year 2000.[186]

Turning to the intended dissemination of lethal biological agents, the last two decades have endured a lot of activity here both within and across nations.[187] In 1984 the Rajneeshee religious cult executed a plan to spread salmonella typhimurium in ten restaurants in rural Oregon, affecting 751 people with food poisoning, and also tried to contaminate the local water supply. In the mid-1980s the Tamil secessionist group in Sri Lanka threatened to infect humans and crops with deadly pathogens. Prior to the 1991 Persian Gulf War, Iraq tested a remote-control fighter plane designed to disperse biological agents, and the nation has admitted to stockpiling anthrax, botulinum toxin, aflatoxin, ricin, and gas gangrene. But perhaps the most important single incident was the attack by the Aum Shinrikyo cult on the Tokyo subway on March 18, 1995 using sarin, a toxic chemical agent, and resulting in twelve dead and 5,000 injured. Not as widely known was the group's keen interest in bioterrorism, involving the purchase of a 48,000-acre area in Australia to test biological agents on livestock; the travel by members to Africa to obtain samples of the lethal Ebola virus; the building of two major research centers in Japan to study biological agents; and the attempted execution of at least four separate bioterrorist strikes prior to the Tokyo subway attack (including ones on New York and Washington, D.C.). This last case illustrates the true cross-national security risks involved in this type of ominous transnational flow.

SECURITY IMPLICATIONS

The security implications of the deadly transfer of infectious diseases are relatively clear-cut—human life is directly threatened. The rapid recent transmission of dangerous microbes seemingly immune to treatment has caused some analysts to call infectious diseases "potentially the largest threat to human security lurking in the post–Cold War world."[188] A 1996 Defense Department report concluded that modern-day terrorist groups have such ready availability of lethal biological agents that they may pose a more likely security threat than that of stolen nuclear material.[189] While the transmission of infectious diseases threatens more the survival of individual human beings than the continuity of political regimes, its dangerous repercussions are extremely difficult to isolate. A major problem posed right off the bat for national defense is that the incubation period for many of these infectious parasitic diseases is over 21 days, making airport surveillance "grossly inadequate" and "often biologically irrational."[190] Moreover, global vulnerability to the spread of infectious diseases is extremely high because of the scarcity of laboratories around the world capable of identifying and managing emerging security threats in this area.[191]

Meanwhile, the dangers of offensive use of infectious diseases and biological agents are growing, as the technology for dispersal becomes more sophisticated, their production becomes easier (especially covertly) and cheaper, and a set of states with questionable regimes—including China, Iran, Iraq, Libya, North Korea, Russia, and Syria—have embarked on offensive biological weapons programs.[192] Many analysts worry that even a well-planned hoax about deadly transfers of infectious diseases would cause a security predicament because of the mass panic and confusion that might ensue.[193] Even the American Medical Association, a staid organization if ever there was one, has become quite alarmed about the security dangers posed by the dangerous link between infectious diseases and biological weapons.[194] The escalating threat here is twofold: a pervasive fear of contracting diseases can combine with a widespread actual loss of life to immobilize a society. This deadly transfer represents one of the few areas where the sense of imminent threat is less a function of actual past oc-

currences and more a product of thinking about apocalyptic outcomes from possible future transactions.

One of the scariest aspects of the security predicament surrounding the deadly transfer of infectious diseases is that an open
international system makes it functionally impossible to prevent
dangerous microbes from spreading across national boundaries.
More than any of the other ominous transnational flows, national
security policy makers find themselves without means at their disposal to attack the problem: neither laws nor detection systems
nor threats of coercive retaliation make a bit of difference in most
cases in slowing down the spread of parasitic infection. The idea
of a true quarantine in today's world makes little sense, as it seems
futile for people to attempt to protect themselves from the inevitable dangerous contacts. No longer can most of the world comfort
itself with the notion that infectious parasitic diseases will mostly
hit so-called "high-risk" populations, such as prostitutes, intravenous drug users, and the like, leaving the rest of the population
largely untouched. Even though the potential for the outbreak of
infectious diseases is still greatest among the poor,[195] the rich cannot find ways to keep from contracting them as well.

When a toxic infectious disease transmitted across national
boundaries personally afflicts a human being, one's short-term reaction seems likely to involve an infuriated sense of panic and
demand for immediate remedies. However, more than with the
other deadly transfers it seems possible in many parts of the world
that the long-term mass reaction to contracting infectious diseases
would be a fatalistic acceptance of the seemingly random vulnerability derived from being in the wrong place at the wrong time,
with little expectation for government protection. Within this open
international system, the advanced industrialized world and the
Third World appear to have two distinctly different modes of reaction to the security threat posed by life-threatening epidemics.
Using AIDS as an example, "in industrialized nations, it is treated
with expensive drug regimens as a 'manageable' chronic condition," whereas "in poorer nations—where more than 90 percent
of all cases occur—infection still means gradual wasting and
death."[196] Given the poor sanitation in much of the Third World
and the consequent prevalence of tuberculosis, dysentery, and res-
piratory infections, there is greater acceptance of poor health and
disease as a normal state of affairs than in industrialized states.

As with the deadly transfer of unsanctioned hazardous materials, the primary thrust of the ominous transnational flow of infectious diseases appears to be endangering the security protection goal of biological survival. Perhaps more directly than any of the other flows, infectious diseases have the capacity to end the life of completely innocent bystanders on the global playground. Equally important, a much larger number of exposed people may not die but will experience extraordinary pain, suffering, and often permanent debilitation as a result of this deadly transfer. Furthermore, those unexposed may live in constant fear of contamination, with absolutely no way to find meaningful security here for themselves and their loved ones. While the other protection goals of political authority and socioeconomic cohesion are not directly affected by the transnational flow of infectious diseases, if a sufficiently large or important segment of a nation's citizenry is hit by an epidemic, then an entire country's political, economic, and social system can grind to a halt.

Chapter 9

Information Disruption Flows

Throughout the global playground, one of the biggest challenges is that of effective communication. In a rowdy and noisy environment, it is easy to misunderstand or not hear others while others are not understanding and not hearing you. On an international level there is a similarity here to a "Tower of Babel" setting, in which everyone is speaking to each other using a different language, dialect, or intonation, and no one is comprehending anything. In a tightly interdependent playground, fragile communication links develop among crucial players that are quite easy to disrupt in such a context. The bullies and ruffians on the playground enjoy such disruption because it increases the sense of anarchy conducive to their uncontrolled behavior and thwarts any effort to develop coordinated coherent unilateral or multilateral strategies promoting security on the global playground. Operating in secret and needing only a few resources, these unruly players find that even the most complex information system is vulnerable to disruption, distortion, and eradication. Rationalizing to themselves that they are not harming any person but rather just demonstrating their cleverness and power by breaking computer security codes, the perpetrators of this deadly transfer are among the most arrogant and irresponsible players on the global playground.

SCOPE OF THE PROBLEM

In recent decades there has been a growing obsession with the security of vital information banks and communications systems linked to national defense. Symptomatic of the escalation of this concern was the release of the movie *War Games* in 1983 depicting fictionally the ease of breaking into Pentagon security systems. Often called information warfare or "cyberterrorism," this deadly transfer somewhat parallels that of infectious diseases: instead of biological viruses threatening human survival, here we face computer viruses (along with other disruptive techniques) threatening the functioning of information systems and ultimately authority structures. Of all the ominous transnational flows discussed in this study, this one appears to have involved most heavily perpetration by deviant individuals (rather than rogue states, terrorist groups, and criminal organizations).

Because the heightened security concern about information disruptions is more recent than any of the other deadly transfers discussed here, an exceptional amount of ambiguity surrounds its definition. A sound general starting point for interpreting this flow is to realize that its mantle includes corrupting, overwhelming, distorting, and leaking vital information or information systems in such a way as to endanger national or global security. A report prepared for the Defense Department entitled *Information Warfare for Dummies: A Guide for the Perplexed* elaborates on this definition by including insertion of malicious code, theft of information, manipulation of information, and denial of service.[197] A major recent study of "cyberspace" threats more specifically details the spectrum of hostile information actions as including "inserting false data or harmful programs into information systems; stealing valuable data or programs from a system, or even taking over control of its operation; manipulating the performance of a system, by changing data or programs, introducing communications delays, etc.; and disrupting the performance of a system, by causing erratic behavior or destroying data or programs, or by denying access to the system."[198] The specific means by which these disruptions are undertaken usually involves "computer attacks" where hackers gain access to a network as legitimate users and then proceed to steal good data, leave bad data behind, insert viruses, flood the system with messages (overwhelming it), or crash the system; all this can be accomplished with cheap equipment, readily-available tools, and "virtually non-existent" risk of detection.[199]

Despite the constantly changing nature of information disruptions linked to the constantly evolving state of information technology, it is possible from these definitions to obtain a relatively clear picture of the parameters of this deadly transfer. It is evident that information disruption includes internal as well as external interference, and that such disruption can be unintentional as well as intentional. This ominous transnational flow is distinctive from the others in that rather than primarily transferring something dangerous from place to place, it serves mainly to prevent the transmission of something really beneficial within and across states. Information disruption can address data themselves or the vital communications systems in which data are embedded; it can remove data, distort data, or add data; and it can eliminate communication, distort communication, add noise to a communication system, or even expand communication to include undesired parties. As immediate, accurate electronic communication becomes increasingly essential to the multifaceted and interdependent command-and-control structures of modern military defense systems, even a modest form of information disruption that simply involves a slight delay in the transmission of vital communication can be sufficient to render an entire security structure ineffective.

The random and sporadic nature of these information break-ins, augmented by the obviously highly classified nature of their overall pattern, makes it impossible to estimate accurately the full global frequency and impact of this ominous transnational flow. However, the experience of the American military, with its more than 2 million computers and more than 10,000 local area networks, gives a troubling indication of the pervasiveness of the problem: in 1995 alone the Pentagon logged more than 250,000 attacks on non-classified computer systems, and in more than 60 percent of the cases the hackers succeeded in penetrating the system.[200] The costs of this kind of disruption are measured not only by the physical damage done to the information systems but also by the money spent on attempting to prevent it from occurring;

one sign of the high toll here is a 1997 recommendation by the Defense Science Board that the Defense Department augment its current information warfare budget of less than $1 billion with an additional $3 billion over the next five years, largely for defensive purposes.[201]

RECENT HISTORY

Two revolutions are involved in the historical origins of the concern about incapacitating information disruptions: the revolution in military affairs, which has turned attention away from traditional declared wars with standing armies to new forms of unconventional conflict; and the information revolution, which has dramatically increased our dependence on data and computers to prepare for and fight wars. The result of these two trends is that "warfare is no longer primarily a function of who puts the most capital, labor and technology on the battlefield, but of who has the best information about the battlefield."[202] While "information has been associated with power, war, and the state since at least the time of the Greek gods,"[203] the global openness and free access to information in the post–Cold War environment is unprecedented in human history, and as a result seems likely to cause "substantial discomfort" through its highlighting of the tensions between security and freedom.[204] Moreover, with the flood of information, "power is migrating to small, nonstate actors who can organize into sprawling networks more readily than can traditional hierarchical nation-state actors."[205] The net result of these recent trends is to make the major status quo global information systems, particularly those possessed by major power states, more vulnerable to disruption from ominous transnational flows.

Although no single incident has been particularly memorable, a large number of anecdotally related cases of the deadly transfer of information disruption serve to illustrate the dangers involved. The perpetrators of the disruptions that follow are quite diverse, as these activities require no more than "a powerful computer, a keen mind, and an underlying grudge."[206] The deviant assortment includes "hackers, zealots or disgruntled insiders, to satisfy personal agendas; criminals, for personal financial gain, etc.; terrorists or other malevolent groups, to advance their cause; commercial organizations, for industrial espionage or to disrupt competitors; nations, for espionage or economic advantage or as a tool of warfare."[207]

Specific post–Cold War information disruption incidents with the United States as a target include Dutch hackers penetrating the Pentagon's computers and offering to sell plans for troop movements to Iraq during Operation Desert Storm in 1991; Russian criminals illegally transferring huge sums of money from Citibank into accounts abroad in 1995; German hackers selling classified American intelligence to the successors of the KGB in 1995 and 1996; and hackers wishing to make a political statement ending up shutting down the Central Intelligence Agency web site in September 1996.[208] Of course, the United States is by no means alone as a target: two illustrative, widely-reported incidents are the revelations in June 1996 that several London financial institutions had for three years been paying huge sums to international criminals who had penetrated their computers and convincingly threatened to shut down the systems unless they received the money; and the report in June 1998 that a group of hackers from the United States, England, Holland, and New Zealand had managed to break into India's national security computer network and steal sensitive nuclear weapons secrets. These disruptive incidents clearly represent the tip of the iceberg for this deadly transfer.

SECURITY IMPLICATIONS

The security priority of incapacitating information disruptions has been escalating rapidly. Central Intelligence Agency John Deutch announced in 1996 that cyberspace attack is one of the top threats to American security, behind only the threat of weapons of mass destruction and the proliferation of nuclear, chemical, and biological weapons.[209] In 1996, President Clinton called for an interconnected "cyber-system" that would provide early warning and minimize damage of attacks on computers controlling the stock market, banking, utilities, air traffic, and other "critical infrastructure" information banks.[210] Two principal reasons why the American defense community is so interested in the ominous flow of information disruptions are that (1) "the United States, in civilian as well as military matters, is more dependent on electronic information systems than is anyone else in the world" and that (2) that information warfare "may be as much an opportunity as it is a threat."[211]

Many analysts are now arguing that disrupting security information systems, rather than attacking traditional military targets, will become the primary thrust of future wars. If each system "becomes the center of gravity for modern militaries, it becomes the logical target of others," and for this reason "information warfare is often cited as the *leitmotif* of early 21st century conflict."[212] The incentives to disrupt one's enemies' defense information systems are identical to those for protecting one's own systems: "as everyone becomes increasingly dependent on automated information systems, the value of maintaining and securing them rises; conversely, the value to an adversary of gaining access to the system, denying service and corrupting its contents, also rises."[213]

Outside of the military security context, the deadly transfer of information disruptions can incapacitate a country in other ways. When transnational criminal organizations undertake such activity, they "pose grave threats to the integrity of the world financial system, undermine the ability of states to protect their citizens, and are themselves a major threat to human rights."[214] This "illicit financial community" steals about $10 billion a year from American financial institutions alone, and with ever-expanding monetary resources "will capitalize on its current strategic advantage and provide a greater challenge to the stability of financial institutions worldwide" by using the Internet to move money quickly to virtual banks in offshore havens outside the reach of national authorities.[215] These criminal activities represent a classic case of distortion, manipulation, and even outright falsification of data that ultimately is highly disruptive to the functioning of civil society in a more bottom-up manner than intrusions into defense communication systems.

The vulnerability to information disruption has proven particularly difficult to overcome. This disruption is extremely difficult to deter because attackers may be anonymous and, even if perpetrators are identified, it is difficult (even more so than many other deadly transfers) to develop effective retaliatory options.[216] Because "defense, the police, banking, trade transportation, scientific work, and a large percentage of the government's and the private sector's transactions are on-line," the result is exposure of "enormous vital areas of national life to mischief or sabotage by any computer hacker, and concerted sabotage could render a country unable to function."[217] Indeed, an American intelligence official has claimed that with $1 billion and 20 capable hackers he could "shut down America."[218] Of all the ominous flows discussed in this study, information is the least expensive and resource-hungry, the most easily transportable, and the most diffusive and hardest to contain, and as a result the potential for information disruption can end up "weakening traditional hierarchical structures" and "eroding some traditional prerogatives of national sovereignty."[219]

One of the most common means of attempting to defend against the security vulnerability here has been the development of encryption technologies. Encryption attempts to protect sensitive information by coding it in such a way that only authorized individuals can determine what the data really mean. Traditionally used by intelligence agencies over the years, encryption has now spread to become commonplace in a wide array of government and financial service organizations. Unfortunately, encryption is a two-edged sword, and transnational criminal organizations have become at least as adept at it as those institutions they attack, with a growth in their use of encryption estimated at between 50 and 100 percent a year: "encryption compounds the problem of the original illicit activity by making it even more difficult to trace the proceeds of the crime or to unravel the records needed to investigate and prosecute the offender," and thus "perpetrators are able to operate with impunity because the significant human and financial resources needed to decode encrypted messages ensure that the investment will be made only for the most important cases."[220] Most targets of this disruptive use of encryption are unable to defend themselves against it, as the National Research Council recently argued that "current U.S. encryption policy is inadequate to meet the increased need for information security," and as a result the technique has been effectively used to deny access to records of deadly transfers of all sorts, including drug shipments and transnational terrorist activities.[221]

In the end, it is worth noting that an uncontrollable flow of massive quantities of sensitive information across national borders can be just as debilitating as having that flow interrupted. While most of the media and government attention has been directed at information disruptions through hacking into important systems and disabling them, the specter of destroying a classified defense information system by leaking out critical pieces of data would be just as damaging, has probably occurred with about equal frequency, and is just as difficult to safeguard. Either way, national security is severely compromised.

More than any of the other deadly transfers, information disruptions directly undermine the security protection goal of political authority. The potential impact on the other protection goals of biological survival and socioeconomic cohesion seems tightly intertwined with issues of authority, as dangers that ensue in these areas would appear to be largely a product of the breakdown in authority structures such as government agencies, banks, and social service organizations. All systems of authority rely on command-and-control systems to function, relying on database management and effective communication among components as the means of keeping track of what is going on, making decisions, and providing necessary services. National defense systems in particular are heavily dependent on this kind of elaborate network to provide an early warning of any impending danger and to formulate quick and effective responses. In recent years, because of the technological breakthroughs in the computer industry, the vast majority of this information is stored electronically, and the vast majority of this communication is done electronically. But the very features that make this electronic authority structure so efficient at the same time make it extremely penetrable.

Chapter 10

National Hypocrisy and Deadly Transfers

To what extent have national governments undertaken whole-hearted, sincere efforts to respond to the challenges posed by these ominous transnational flows? Unfortunately, government policies addressing these transactions appear to exhibit considerable ambivalence, inconsistency, and downright hypocrisy.[222] It is certainly unreasonable to expect national policy on these flows to be perfectly coherent across time and geographical areas, especially given that these transactions are deeply embedded in a large and complex set of domestic and foreign problems; however, state responses—particularly those of industrialized nations—to the flows considered here seem in many ways to exceed the normal threshold for embodying contradictory tendencies. While some of the inconsistency here is clearly a product of the web of other issues involved, in many cases corruption, greed, shortsightedness, ignorance, or fatalistic acceptance appear to play a role in government officials' hypocrisy regarding these transactions.

With respect to conventional arms, where perhaps the clearest inconsistency exists, industrialized nations' governments openly state that they are adamantly opposed to conventional arms proliferation for security reasons, while privately permitting, encouraging, and even participating in the covert sale of their weapons systems and components abroad through direct and indirect channels for economic reasons. The rhetoric of restraint ("we are opposed to indiscriminate conventional arms sales"), order ("we sell weapons only to our friends"), and security ("military assistance helps to enhance military deterrence and to stabilize alliances") appears to clash with the reality of expansiveness ("we need to help our defense industry achieve global market penetration"), chaos ("if we don't permit sales to them, someone else will"), and profit ("arms sales provide jobs and income for our citizenry"). There is an underlying tension between idealism and realism evident here: the governmental justification for arms transfers usually revolves around the altruistic motives of promoting security, stability, and peace, when actually they result more from a pragmatic emphasis on "economic advantage and political expediency."[223] Supplier states appear to be trapped between the utility of the public good and the attractiveness of private gain.

Regarding illegal migration, industrialized nations' governments have voiced increasing opposition to this flow and increasing commitment to stop it in order to maintain the security of their citizenry, while at the same time they have repeatedly not tightly enforced existing regulations, not imposed strict penalties, and not properly restricted offers of asylum when their own companies have privately arranged to import cheap illegal aliens for economic profit.[224] An underlying ambivalence exists about how much government time and effort ought to be spent trying to keep out those who seem to want desperately to come to one's country and who seem to have a beneficial role to play—at least in the short term—in one's economy. Increasing enforcement of restrictions aimed at illegal migrants can stir up charges of nativism, activate citizen groups originally from the same home country and their sympathizers, and amplify domestic ethnic and racial tensions; so for many states with highly permeable borders the questionable payoff from coherently-applied sanctions against illegal aliens does not appear to them to justify the high costs.

Moving to illicit drugs, industrialized states' governments have expressed grave concern about drug trafficking due to its dire security implications; but in practice defense agencies have been reluctant to participate in the war on drugs,[225] and consuming state governments often functionally tolerate or under-punish the use of illegal drugs because of either the widespread social demand for them or the economic profits deriving from their sale. In the United States, the originator of the war on drugs, impediments to more effective illicit drug policy at home and abroad also include bureaucratic wrangling and clashes with values related to protecting human rights, reinforcing civilian democracies, and promoting regional stability.[226] Drug-producing states share as well in this atmosphere of hypocrisy: "attempts to repress the drug trade in the Andean countries have also been dogged by corruption and lack of political will,"[227] a predicament that may very well derive from contradictions between domestic interests involved in drug production and the official state policy formulated in response to pressures from North America.[228]

Turning to unsanctioned hazardous materials, industrialized states' governments have repeatedly uttered general disapproval of the transboundary movement of both conventional hazardous wastes and dangerous nuclear materials because of the security threat to human life, but these nations have been quite lax in strictly enforcing regulatory controls, in establishing globally effective bans on the transmission of such toxic materials, and in finding better ways of monitoring the cross-border movement of these substances. These deficiencies are largely due to the economic profits generated and the pervasive "not-in-my-backyard" syndrome.[229] The U.S. government has been among the most vigorous in attempting to clean up its own contaminated land, yet—seemingly ignoring the idea that recipient nations might have the same desires—it has simultaneously been the largest producer and exporter of hazardous waste.[230] In the short run, of course, this contradiction is largely invisible, as a kind of "blissful ignorance"[231] often exists about the long-term, harmful side effects of hazardous materials transfers.

Looking at infectious diseases, industrialized states' governments have consistently expressed deep fear of both the unintentional spread of viruses and the intentional transmission of biological agents, and yet the amount of resources these governments actually allocate to monitor and manage these ominous transnational flows is miniscule. While the annual number of people afflicted with infectious diseases is much greater than that of all the casualties of military combat in the 1990s, "global public expenditures on the war against disease are a pittance compared to military expenditures."[232] A study in 1995 by the World Health Organization (WHO) of the international capability for identifying and addressing disease threats revealed disturbing results: only six laboratories in the world met security and safety standards for research on the deadliest microbes; and of these sites two (in Russia) were jeopardized by local political instability and three (two in the United States, including the Centers for Disease Control, and one in Britain) were jeopardized by budget cuts.[233] On another occasion WHO sent samples of the world's deadliest diseases to the 35 leading global disease-monitoring facilities, only to discover that just one—the Centers for Disease Control—diagnosed them all correctly, and most got over half wrong.[234] Once again, the gap between the rhetoric of security alarm and the reality of action in terms of expenditure is sizable, with other economic priorities clearly taking precedence.

Finally, concluding with incapacitating information disruptions, industrialized states' governments repeatedly decry break-ins to their own defense security systems as heinous, criminal, and barbaric; yet these same governments are quite at home with using these same potentially unethical information disruption methods against others. Even if issues of ethics were ignored, the tightly interconnected global communication and information links would appear to make it counterproductive for everyone to have information warfare be a normal, accepted mode of interaction. For example, the officially sanctioned information warfare doctrine for the U.S. Air Force (the branch of the armed services most concerned about information disruption) includes a section advocating the "targeting of the enemy's information and information functions," through exploiting, corrupting, or destroying its information systems, "with the intent of degrading his will or capacity to fight."[235] While this prescription makes complete sense from the point of view of military strategy, it appears to be highly inconsistent with comments by national leaders about the uncivilized nature of information disruption flows in a tightly interdependent and fragile global communications system. Moreover, government initiatives have been largely half-hearted up to this point to protect vital information systems from the deadly transfer of being "hacked, tapped, penetrated, bugged, and infected with computer viruses" associated with efforts from our adversaries abroad; this lack of full-scale action is due not only to political freedom-of-expression resistance from the civilian information structure but also to economic free-market resistance from those inside and outside of government who see safeguards against information disruption decreasing economic efficiency.[236]

Within each of these flows, a significant clash exists between publicly stated rhetoric largely motivated by security concerns and privately practiced action heavily motivated by economic concerns. It is certainly possible to argue that this inconsistency is not particularly novel or unexpected because only a narrow range of elites would notice it, and that those who did recognize it would be so cynical that they would largely accept such contradictory tendencies. Indeed, onlookers inside and outside of nations have seemed to react in a jaded and unconcerned manner when their governments have experienced humiliating scandals that should in many ways be far more devastating than little inconsistencies in dealing with deadly transfers.

Moreover, it would seem foolish to argue that a complete elimination of inconsistency and hypocrisy within national governmental responses to the deadly transfers would be the central ingredient in a strategy to reduce the prevalence of these transactions. Lethargic, overworked, or distracted government officials may simply be focusing on other issues that are more pressing at the moment, not consciously attempting to maintain a two-faced foreign defense policy (thus making the label of hypocrisy off-base and far too condemning). National governments need to maintain flexibility in being able to create different kinds of security policies to deal with widely differing kinds of threats, even when from the outside these policies may appear to be contradictory. Sensitive protection of national interests frequently involves balancing competing domestic and foreign concerns that entail considerable expedient compromise rather than rigid adherence to principle. Placing a straightjacket on our leaders demanding complete symmetry between statements and actions in every case would appear to be a sure way to ensure policy failure.

However, it would appear that for state policy to have any prospect of effectiveness globally in restraining clandestine arms, illegal migration, illicit drugs, hazardous materials, infectious diseases, and information disruptions, it would need to exhibit the kind of coherence and integrity that would send a strong signal through more clearly practicing what it preaches. Thanks to improvements in communication and a growing penchant by the media and transnational watchdog groups (despite their glaring inadequacies mentioned earlier) to unearth government hypocrisy, a growing proportion of the public is slowly becoming a lot more aware of the tensions and contradictions involved in government policy and action regarding the ominous transnational flows. Even more importantly, awareness is growing that the perpetrators of these dangerous transactions benefit from the inconsistency in state policy as the contradictions help to prevent governments from taking united and effective steps to eradicate the problem. It does not seem to matter whether these contradictions are the product of honest, hardworking officials simply facing tradeoffs in national values that are difficult to reconcile, or conversely the product of corrupt, slovenly officials who place personal gain above national interest; in either case, the impact of the hypocrisy seems devastating. In other words, there seems to be little hope for diminished activity by the people who receive and facilitate these transfers if it is clear to them that their governments are not really sure they want to stop these flows.

As mentioned in Chapter 1, playground monitors in today's world are not known for effective, coherent action in managing turmoil within their environment. On the global level, turning a blind eye to disruptive activity that is going on seems just as likely as on local school and park playgrounds, motivated by the same concerns about the uselessness of detecting such behavior: if one has no effective, widely accepted means for stopping the unsanctioned behavior once it is spotted, either because existing punishments do not deter future incidents or because so much of this behavior goes on covertly outside the gaze of monitors, then highlighting the existence of the unruly behavior on the playground serves only to foster widespread fear among potential victims and a pervasive sense that the monitors are both weak and indecisive. Moreover, there is a lemming-like conformity effect here supporting muzzled monitoring with respect to the deadly transfers, as the feeling is prevalent that "no one else is reigning in this activity, so why should I?"; or "if I don't engage in corrupt collusion with the ruffians and bullies, someone else will"; or "making the huge effort to apprehend and punish unruly players will do nothing to stop the dangerous transfers or change the passive behavior of the other monitors."

Thus there is more than a little bit of rationality associated with the seeming hypocrisy of playground monitors and national governments when dealing with ominous flows. It really does take uncharacteristically heroic efforts in today's anarchic global environment to take firm first steps to stunt the growth of the deadly transfers, and the potential for ineffectiveness or boomerang effects really does seem quite large. However, understanding the logic behind the hesitation and inconsistency of national leaders in responding to the deadly transfers is different from condoning it, for to do so would truly allow the bullies and ruffians of the world free reign.

Finally, linking this widespread national hypocrisy to the security protection goals of biological survival, political authority, and socioeconomic cohesion reveals some interesting patterns. It would generally appear that government sincerity in pursuing policies to curtail deadly transfers would be highest (and, consequently, national hypocrisy would be lowest) in dealing with challenges to survival. The primary reason behind this priority would seem to be bottom-up democratic pressures to protect that which the mass public feels is most visibly the central security concern— their own lives. At the same time, however, there may very well be a feeling of governmental helplessness in finding ways to address effectively survival threats from ominous transnational flows: the ability to stop arms, drugs, toxic materials, and infectious diseases from killing people is generally outside of any regime's effective control. With political authority, national governments obviously have a lot they can do, but this is an area of considerable hypocrisy due to the frequent placement (as discussed earlier) of economic profit over political security concerns. As to socioeconomic cohesion, this protection goal appears to lie somewhere in the middle, with not as much governmental influence or national hypocrisy as political authority, but considerably more than biological survival.

Chapter 11

Crippled International Rules of the Game and the Global Playground

To what extent are the ominous transnational flows influenced by the "rules of the game" prevalent in the international system as a whole? Certainly in all cases national laws—and in some cases international agreements—have emerged attempting to restrict these activities. A more probing answer to this question, however, reveals that a breakdown in the post–Cold War global rules of the game has helped to inhibit a truly effective collective response here.[237] The notion of rules of the game in international relations is a long-standing concept reflecting what is implicitly or explicitly permissible in patterns of interaction on the conflict-cooperation continuum.[238] The quagmire surrounding these rules, linked directly to the discussion of the global playground presented earlier, appears to be particularly salient to the security challenges posed by the flows considered in this study.

With the old Cold War rules largely gone, there appears to be little understanding of—or compliance to—a new set of rules. Some have even argued that the international system "changes are so thoroughgoing as to render obsolete the rules and procedures by which politics are conducted."[239] In the absence of a uniform and universal rule-set that is consistently voiced and followed, each actor in the system is free to behave largely according to its own idiosyncratic premises. A common image is that the West plays by the rules, since it sets them, while others are more likely to ignore and violate them; but the reality is that no one consistently plays by a coherent global set of rules, including the West (tying in with the earlier discussion of national hypocrisy).

The West generally assumes its rules are universal, and either projects in a misleading way its rule-set onto others (interpreting others' behavior in terms of its own rules) or attempts to impose directly its rule-set onto others and force compliance. The results here are resentment, misunderstanding, and largely ineffective international initiatives (including those addressing the flows considered in this study). In contrast to many past systems, core powers do not seem to be able to set by themselves the rules of the game, at least in part due to their lack of widespread legitimacy in the global arena, a deficiency that can also increase their vulnerability to the deadly transfers.[240] The West operates as if a mix of military coercion, economic dependence, legal prohibition, and moral outrage will suffice to quell violations of their idea of the rules of the game, a premise that appears particularly flawed when applied to the types of groups that facilitate the dangerous transfers considered here.

With major powers still clinging to a largely outmoded set of rules, weaker states are able to ignore them and non-state groups can subvert them. The increasing popularity of moral relativism, with its premium placed on non-judgmental multicultural patterns of diversity, can cause any discussion of establishing a more coherent set of rules of the game—especially by the West—to run the risk of comparison to the most virulent forms of cultural imperialism; to establish more universal rules in this way of thinking seems to be the equivalent of an anti-democratic squashing of each global actor's ability to experience independent empowerment by defining its own mode of behavior. For the disenfranchised nations, the very notion of rules of the game in today's world is reminiscent of an era where they sacrificed autonomy in their foreign policy for what they perceived to be a quite arbitrary world order. Moreover, for many disadvantaged states and groups that seem permanently unable to be upwardly mobile in the global hierarchy, violating the rules of the game may be a primary means for escaping from a stifling and humiliating status quo, a system whose premises they feel powerless to influence.[241] Actors who do not want to play by the rules, including rogue states, terrorist groups, criminal organizations, and deviant individuals, know that in today's international system it is extremely difficult for major powers to exert effective pressure on them over the long haul to change their behavior, and indeed a significant component of these non-compliant actors' status appears to derive from their ability to thwart in flagrant ways the major powers' rules of the game and to get away with it without suffering devastating consequences. Thus in some ways it is actually useful for these unruly actors to have the West continue to portray its rules as universal so that their defiant power can be ever more visible.

With the global spread of democratic and capitalist beliefs, one might expect common rules of the game to gain both greater coherence and greater acceptance on the international level. Even given nations' very different interpretations of these concepts, it would certainly seem as if the value placed on the responsiveness of the rulers, choice by the ruled, and free open exchange could be a springboard for shared global norms that had considerable meaning and weight. Unfortunately, the newly transplanted post–Cold War political and economic systems frequently deviate considerably from the ideal: "in some countries, the new rulers appear to be not good democrats and legitimate businessmen, as hoped, but a new breed of political-criminal actors and illicit entrepreneurs," with "one form of authoritarianism being replaced by another."[242]

While there is a clearly mutually reinforcing link between state hypocrisy and crippled global rules of the game, the difficulties in responding to the ominous transnational flows are by no means confined to national governments and their interrelationships. Compounding these external impediments are sharp internal divisions within global public opinion, which can be extremely important in this context because compliance to international rules of the game may be heavily affected by domestic policy processes.[243] More specifically, the citizenry of these states is split between (1) those who want to eliminate the flow of clandestine arms, illegal migrants, illicit drugs, hazardous materials, infectious diseases, and information disruptions, and (2) those who want basic freedoms preserved—including those who genuinely desire to consume or utilize what is being transferred covertly—or who profit from these transactions. In most societies this split is a quite hazy and ambiguous one, where the lines between the two sides are not clearly drawn because of the absence of open public debate on the potentially divisive and inflammatory issues linked to the deadly transfers.

Moreover, highly consistent with the global spread of these transactions is the refusal to think about the broad systemic implications of one's own actions among the world's population. Acquiring clandestine arms seems to be an instant remedy to a sense of powerlessness, with recipients able to ignore the more general violent effects associated with the spread of weaponry. Illegally migrating to another country seems to be an instant path to wealth, with undocumented aliens able to ignore the more general economic problems they may create in recipient societies. Indulging in illicit drugs seems to facilitate an instant escape from confronting the depressing realities of one's existence, with users able to ignore the more general breakdown of social structures in consuming nations. Pawning off hazardous materials seems to provide immediate relief from suffering the dangers of one's own toxic contaminants, with transmitting agents able to ignore the more general spillover effects and—in the case of weapons-grade nuclear materials—threats to global survival associated with such transfers. Transmitting biological agents spreading infectious diseases seems to be a speedy means of demonstrating fundamental disapproval of target societies, yet the perpetrators can ignore the inability to contain the impact and the possibility of a global epidemic affecting large numbers of completely innocent people. Finally, disrupting information systems has the potential to paralyze seemingly oppressive power structures, but the initiators ignore how many basic essential services needed by the community at large could be cut off as a result. As long as a substantial portion of the mass public is in a mode where it expects to be able to get whatever it wants wherever and whenever it chooses, regardless of the legality of the transaction, and where the pursuit of power, pleasure, and profit reigns supreme, national governments will be handcuffed in attempts to control these flows.

It appears useful to examine the rules-of-the-game predicament specifically in the playground context. Suppose that, on a given school or park playground, dramatically changing external circumstances rendered previous rules of the game obsolete. The powerful status quo players on the playground who benefited from the old system would assume that they could set the new rules and that these rules would be universal, while many others on the playground—especially new entrants and those who felt the old system was disadvantageous to them—would resent this imposition and resist it. The unruly bullies and ruffians would take advantage of this situation by flaunting their defiance of any emerging set of rules. The onlookers may feel as much unhappiness with the powerful players for being presumptuous in their attempted imposition of authority as with the unruly players for being disruptive in their defiance of authority.

As highlighted by this playground narrative, the underlying problem is that the old set of rules of the game has changed and that a new set has not yet emerged to replace it. Under such circumstances, what would appear to be most effective is not an arrogant, top-down stepping up by the old guard to take control of the situation, but rather a more sensitive, bottom-up development of a new set of rules, involving discussion among key players about what kind of rules are needed under a situation characterized by high flux and uncertainty. Then some common ground rules may emerge that will be perceived as more legitimate and that all may be happier to help enforce because each player senses having a role in their creation and having personal values embedded within them. While consensus on a new set of rules of the game appears to be highly unlikely in a world containing extremely diverse belief systems, some hope exists that recognition of mutual dangers will stimulate some level of grudging agreement. However, what impedes this kind of collective development of rules of the game on the global playground is a combination of mutual distrust, pessimism about the possibility of a common rule-set emerging, and inattention to the severity and immediacy of the broad security dangers posed by the deadly transfers.

To some observers, it may seem odd to be talking about rules of the game on a global playground characterized by chaotic anarchy. Although rules of the game seem much more salient to deadly transfers than the enactment of law or the scheduling of conferences, because rules of the game reflect practical understandings in the minds of the players of the real limits to their behavior, these rules clearly can constitute only a small part of any strategy to address these ominous flows. However, even on the most disorderly setting a functional set of rules exist that the players implicitly recognize. The rules may be as crude as "might makes right," but they nonetheless exist.

The problem comes on the playground, as it does in the international arena, if the monitors believe that there is one set of operative rules and the rest of the players respond to another set that is both different and contradictory to those the monitors talk about. The problem is compounded when the monitors themselves secretly violate the very rules they say should apply on the playground. This inconsistency (fostered by national hypocrisy) makes it more likely that bullies and ruffians who openly defy the stated rules will receive increased admiration from the rest of the players. The monitors' contradictory behavior also reduces the chances that they will ever reach complete agreement in practice on what kind of universal rules of the game should be applied.

When considering the crippled international rules of the game in the context of the protection goals of biological survival, political authority, and socioeconomic cohesion, it might at first seem as if the starting point for establishing a meaningful new set of rules of the game would be survival, since people most immediately recognize this as a primary security concern. Unfortunately, a closer look reveals that this would indeed be a quite problematic place for the international community (as opposed to individual national governments) to begin: protection of human life relates directly to concerns about basic human needs and human rights, and these are areas guarded jealously by national constitutions as crucial defining aspects of state sovereignty. In other words, because the issue of protecting human rights is so fundamental, each nation-state in a rather distinctive way has erected a set of tightly worded principles on its own to safeguard them, and attempting to establish global rules of the game would challenge and demand compromise in these fundamental national principles. It thus appears impossible to address the problem of deadly transfers through a more coherent and widely accepted set of global rules of the game pertaining to biological survival without clashing with these most basic individual rights defined in an idiosyncratic way by each nation. The problem here becomes clearer when one realizes that global rules of the game regarding the ominous transnational flows might entail sacrifices of some cherished personal freedoms, such as the rights to privacy, to move oneself and one's goods freely from place to place, and to express oneself freely in order to detect, apprehend, and prosecute the perpetrators of the deadly transfers.

Turning to political authority, it appears that there is an inherent zero-sum relationship between establishing firm and universally applicable global rules of the game to deal with the deadly transfers and maintaining the central authority of state governments. Unlike biological survival, where the individual must give up rights protected by the state in order to have common global sanctions about protecting human life developed, here it is the state itself that must give up some of its rights. The security sphere, which of course the ominous transnational flows directly fall into, is the one where states most vehemently safeguard their sovereign rights: for example, it is much easier for regional blocs to deal with economic issues than security issues, and many nations (including the United States) have expressed concern on more than one occasion that the United Nations is interfering with their sovereign ability to provide security for their citizenry. The payoffs for this sacrifice of national authority to combat the deadly transfers do not appear very high to most nations of the world, as for the benefit of some idealistic sense of common ground they would bear the cost of not being able to take action in the way they saw fit against foreign perpetrators of the ominous transnational flows within their borders.

Finally, looking at the protection goal of socioeconomic cohesion in relationship to the crippled global rules of the game, the situation regarding deadly transfers is quite different when dealing with the economic components on the one hand and the sociocultural components on the other. While perhaps the greatest progress has occurred in establishing common international ground rules for transnational business, given the global spread of the free-market system and the general acceptance of the open economy and intense competition assumptions that go with it, there is quite a bit of disagreement about whether or not the substances, technologies, and people embedded in the ominous transnational flows ought to be treated in the same way as other commodities. If these dangerous transfers are not to be treated in the same way, then there is huge confusion about how to demarcate the set of special items in this unsanctioned category. Cultural traditions within each country, some of which permit and promote such dangerous activities as violence using arms and the use of illicit drugs, face an even more seemingly insuperable obstacle in terms of global rules of the game—it has been generally accepted for some time that this rule-set has no right to interfere with the lifestyle choices within each state. Of all the three protection goals, having global rules of the game cover internal sociocultural patterns would seem to generate the most immediate and widespread cries of illegitimacy.

Chapter 12

Security Implications— Turning a Playground into a Civil Community

Some lessons emerge from the case studies and the limited national and international success in halting the spread of deadly transfers on the global playground. On the surface, the picture appears more than a bit bleak, as individual action seems inadequate and collective action seems infeasible. With frightened, victimized individuals seemingly more aware of the new dangers on the playground than governing structures, which frequently cling to tired, ineffective rules, antiquated detection systems, and outmoded ideal visions, there appears to be little hope that the common understanding needed to confront successfully the ominous transnational flows will actually emerge.

URGENT FIRST STEPS

Yet there clearly is an urgency to move quickly to begin to establish ways to deal with these problems. If deadly transfers are permitted to proliferate beyond a certain threshold on the global playground, then they will become the new, universally accepted norm. Historical patterns certainly indicate that after a certain penetration—involving high dispersion and high duration—of

arms, drugs, crime, disease, and the like into societies, governments and their citizenry begin to cease to view them as security-
reducing disruptions and begin to adjust to the normalcy of their
continued presence.

An important starting point appears to be to recognize that existing national and global authority structures using standard operating procedures are not likely to be sufficient to manage the
demise of these transactions. To rest confidently with the thought
that everything will work itself out without much reconsideration
of alternative options is to enhance the vulnerability to these ominous flows in the future. The scope of the deadly transfers, in
terms of both the number of states participating in them as initiators and recipients and the depth of penetration into grassroots
activities within these countries, appears to call for some new
strategies. While standard defense mechanisms are frequently
quite capable of managing conventional types of threats, the proliferation of the unorthodox security dangers posed by the ominous transnational flows occurs precisely because the perpetrators
of these transactions have pinpointed the weaknesses of these traditional defensive responses when operating in the open, porous
environment of the global playground.

Given the nature of the security threat posed, it seems inescapable that any solutions (1) should not be strictly top-down or
bottom-up but instead involve joint action undertaken by
governments and their citizenry and (2) should not be local or
unilateral but instead involve joint action undertaken by nations
housing both initiators and recipients of these transactions. At first
glance the spread of the democratic value system across nations
would appear to be conducive to both of these trends, but re-
sponsive pluralistic systems seem to be much better at dealing
with blatant dangers posed by identifiable initiators than at dealing with those posed by covert flows undertaken on the sly. More
widespread understanding of the deadly transfer phenomenon itself appears to be the only route capable of overcoming this stymieing of joint action.

A cornerstone needed to expand this understanding of the
deadly transfers is to recognize that traditional forms of intelligence have not been and will not be adequate to track these kinds
of covert transnational flows. Although the intelligence community has made major strides in tracking the behavior of rogue

states and terrorist groups, it is only beginning to become adept at following closely the movement of internationally disruptive activities by criminal organizations and deviant individuals. While today it seems hard to believe, it was not until September 1995 that the Central Intelligence Agency, under pressure from Congress, "agreed to include the investigation and infiltration of global criminal gangs as part of its mission."[244] Domestic intelligence agencies such as the Federal Bureau of Investigation are far more used to covering these last two sets of players than foreign intelligence agencies such as the Central Intelligence Agency; but a long tradition exists in this country and elsewhere of poor information-sharing between local law enforcement operations and international intelligence operations.[245] The expanding scope of activity by criminal organizations and deviant individuals on the global playground appears to require an explicitly international intelligence thrust. Moreover, while in recent years intelligence agencies have followed more carefully transnational shipment of clandestine arms, transmission of illicit drugs, and movement of illegal migrants, there has still been relatively little intelligence attention paid to the deadly transfers of hazardous materials (though the movement of nuclear components has drawn considerable notice), infectious diseases (though a flood of recent concern has surrounded the spread of biological agents), and information disruptions. A reorientation of intelligence seems crucial at the outset because, before new strategies can emerge to address the deadly transfers, a more comprehensive and accurate awareness of the scope and nature of the problem—far beyond what current anecdotal evidence can provide—must exist.

There has usually been a sizable gap between calling for a reorientation of intelligence and actually detailing how it ought to be altered. Although a comprehensive plan is well beyond the scope of this study, a few general ideas seem worth noting. Perhaps the first question is: What do we need to know about the deadly transfers? Aside from having a more systematic picture of the scope and nature of these flows, nations need to have much better knowledge about the strength of the perpetrators, their goals, plans, and intentions, and the actual impact on them of decisions and actions taken to halt the ominous transnational flows.[246] To accomplish these information acquisition tasks, it is absolutely clear than human intelligence (rather than technical intelligence gathered through electronic means) is most vital,[247] as the concealed nature of the deadly transfers makes them difficult to spot even at close range. It is equally apparent that secure sharing of intelligence among relevant agencies both within and across states is essential to track these elusive transactions. While expecting direct penetration and infiltration of the leadership of rogue states, terrorist groups, criminal organizations, and deviant individuals' support circles seems a bit unrealistic, it does not seem unreasonable to expect that newly targeted intelligence could do better at getting second-hand information about these perpetrators of the ominous transnational flows.

WHY NOT JUST FURTHER EMPOWER THE MONITORS?

However, one immediate question arises upon considering this set of transformational issues—why not just increase the number and power of the monitors on the global playground to solve the deadly transfers problem? If there were more monitors to spot this activity, if they had in hand more rules and regulations about what kinds of activities were prohibited, and if they possessed means of immediate enforcement of these sanctions, would not the problem be solved? Unfortunately, the predicament here is not nearly that simple.

First, as alluded to in Chapter 1, there is a motivational issue about the incentives for the monitors (no matter how many of them there are) to spot the ominous flows and to enforce existing rules (no matter how clear the regulations are). Frequently, identifying troublemakers and apprehending them creates a whole new set of problems that monitors would prefer to avoid, and in any case—particularly on the global level—the interests of these troublemakers and the interests of some of the monitors may coincide or may be artificially induced to coincide (through bribery and corruption). Second, even untainted monitors may honestly believe that the so-called deadly transfers are not really so dangerous to society as a whole (as opposed to the initiators and recipients themselves) and are generally innocuous. Third, even the best monitoring system would have difficulty detecting many of these deadly transfers, given that many of them are functionally invisible and are handled through seemingly legitimate enterprises. Fourth, in practice on the global level there would be considerable difficulty getting agreement among all the monitors about what the rules should be and what they really mean (discussed in Chapter 11), as nations around the world have very different policies about outlawed transactions in arms, drugs, migrants, hazardous materials, and the like. Finally, because of issues of state sovereignty, empowering an international set of monitors in this way would end up escalating jurisdictional squabbles about who had the right to prosecute and punish the troublemakers.

Looking at the practical limitations facing the actual monitors of this activity—national governments, international organizations, and transnational watchdog groups—helps to illustrate the realistic deficiencies of attempting to address the deadly transfers primarily by empowering the monitors. National governments are most hampered by the basic safeguards on freedom provided in most states of the world espousing democratic principles, and a turn toward vigorous apprehension and prosecution of initiators and recipients of the ominous transnational flows can create major internal dissention. Raising the issue of the deadly transfers in an international organization like the United Nations can serve to highlight painful differences in interpretation and an unwillingness to modify national regulations to conform a global standard. Finally, transnational watchdog groups tend to have narrow segmented agendas, making it difficult for any of them to address effectively the full interlocked spectrum of deadly transfers operating on the global level.

Even more fundamentally, as demonstrated in Chapter 3, a basic problem exists in attempting to use deterrence-oriented coercion as a principal means for discouraging rogue states, terrorist groups, criminal organizations, and deviant individuals from engaging in deadly transfers. Increasing the number and power of playground monitors inevitably relies on the threat of detection and punishment as the means of restraint, and in the specific context of the deadly transfers the effectiveness of threatening the use of retaliatory force has been consistently shown to be highly questionable. While to discard deterrence completely as a means of confronting the deadly transfers on the global playground would obviously be foolhardy, it seems impossible to place one's entire trust in a doctrine that is clearly ill-suited to the task. One must be careful not to "throw out the baby with the bath water" here—just because increasing the number and power of playground monitors should not be the primary avenue to eliminate the deadly transfers, that does not mean that monitors should be eliminated altogether or even considered for reduction. On the international level, credible monitoring of the ominous transnational flows and reasonable enforcement powers to deal with perpetrators seems to be a crucial prerequisite to any solution. But while this is a necessary ingredient in any strategy to counter the deadly transfers, it is by no means sufficient, and it has dominated far too much the thinking of security policy makers as the only response to take.

GENERAL OBSTACLES TO PROGRESS

Right now the largest obstacle to addressing the deadly transfers appears to be the huge perceptual distance between what most individuals, groups, and nations want for themselves and what kind of negative impact they think fulfilling those desires would have on society as a whole: they not only focus on the benefits to themselves far more than the costs to society, but in many cases they deny that these societal costs are even created or are worth caring about at all. To be perfectly frank, it appears that many members of the general public have not yet fully come to grips with changes in the context in which their actions take place—the absence of the "peace dividend" and a stable "new world order" after the end of the Cold War and the presence instead of volatile and violent anarchy on a global scale. So what is needed most is not only an increased sensitivity to societal costs but also a heightened awareness both that pursuit of the benefits of immediate self-gratification can directly create these costs and—even more importantly from a self-interest standpoint—that the societal costs can prevent the secure enjoyment of the individual benefits. Ultimately only through an attitude change reflecting this sensitivity and awareness can the gap begin to shrink between what one thinks is best for oneself and what one thinks is best for the community.

Some troublesome patterns seem evident revolving around these perceptions by citizens and their governments about deadly transfers and the three security protection goals discussed in this study—biological survival, political authority, and socioeconomic cohesion. As might be expected, the greatest unity among members of the mass public revolves around deadly transfers affecting their own survival because of the immediacy of the threat.[248] As discussed in Chapter 10, although national governmental hypocrisy may be lowest in dealing with survival issues, this area may be the one that states are least capable of effectively addressing in today's porous international system. So an undesirable situation seems to emerge here with respect to the deadly transfers in which the mass public may be expecting and demanding most from the government precisely what government officials may feel they are least capable of successfully addressing. The net result of this predicament has been, of course, for citizens frustrated with the lack of effective action from their governments to try to take protection from the deadly transfers into their own hands, thus increasing the focus on self-interest rather than community interest.

As states become increasingly aware of their vulnerability to these ominous transactions, national governments face intensifying cross-cutting pressures from within and without, leading to more finger pointing and tensions both among governments and between a government and its people. Because of the complex nature of the bidirectional movement of the six deadly transfers, discussed in Chapter 2, security tensions between developed and developing states appear to be particularly likely, with neither side able to claim any moral high ground with respect to its innocence in stimulating these transactions. Moreover, the deadly transfers clearly have the potential to skew aid and dependency relationships between these sending and receiving states,[249] complicating any attempt to justify resulting alliances. A similar predicament seems likely within countries, as neither the citizenry nor the government has completely clean hands, and each feels the other should be more responsible in solving the deadly transfer problem. In the end, it appears that the ambiguity of sources of these dangerous transactions (with each side able to claim with some credibility that it is not really responsible for the problem) serves to increase the unmanageable stress confronting national governments.

Under these domestic and international pressures, state regimes may find themselves experiencing declining capacities to govern and possessing declining legitimacy,[250] fueling "a growing privatization of security and violence—in the form of legions of private security guards, the proliferation of small arms among the general population, and the spread of vigilante and 'self-defense' groups."[251] As the established monitors on the global playground become regarded as ineffective, the players will begin to supplant them with monitors of their own choosing, creating even more diversity in rules and enforcement systems used. While national governments' armies have shrunken in size since the end of the Cold War from 28.7 million uniformed troops in 1988 to 23 million in 1995, private security forces have been on the rise: "in several countries, private security forces rival or outstrip the size of the public police, and in some—among them Australia, South Africa, and the United States—they outnumber even the national army"; one report even claims that "gun-toting" private guards in the United States "have more firepower than the combined police forces of the nation's 30 largest urban centers."[252] This privatization trend would seem to play right into the hands of those facilitating the deadly transfers.

In the broadest sense, these flows place national governments in a real international relations bind. Basic value clashes between individual freedom and collective order, between economic profit and political security, and between openness and protection help prevent the formulation and implementation of strong sanctions here. The tensions among the basic values identified by this discussion of deadly transfers on the global playground serve to highlight fundamental internal ambiguities within the precepts of both democracy and capitalism when operating in the peculiar post–Cold War environment. These clashes serve to paralyze policy-making initiatives until or unless a government and its citizens begin to grapple directly with the contradictions involved.

The tensions between individual freedom and collective order connect to the tradeoffs involved in the choice between pursuing justice and pursuing stability. As the threat from the deadly transfers increases, the pressures within states intensify to downplay the former in order to achieve the latter end. This stability emphasis, preserving existing authority structures and the integrity of national boundaries in the face of disruptive turmoil generated by the ominous transnational flows, seems intrinsically problematic in a rapidly changing world: the legitimacy of these structures and boundaries often seems quite arbitrary when looked at in broad historical perspective;[253] and a focus on stability is likely to lead to disappointment due to the need for continuing adaptation and movement.[254] Yet if one considers the alternative emphasis on justice, promoting the rights of individuals and groups, then the specter emerges of inadvertently facilitating violent chaos associated with the deadly transfers by reducing the ability of a government to monitor the behavior of its citizenry.

The tensions between profit and security relate directly to the need for recognition of the tradeoffs in today's world between gaining narrow material benefits for oneself and contributing broad benefits to the greater community. Those who support an "economics first" approach to foreign defense policy often do so because they deny this tradeoff and do not see the deadly transfers as a strategically crucial issue due to their gross underestimation of the threat posed to their country.[255] This false sense of confidence allows many inappropriately to characterize the pursuit of profit through the facilitation of all kinds of cross-national transactions to be perfectly harmonious with security welfare.

The tensions between openness and protection reflect perhaps the most fundamental tradeoff in today's highly globalized interdependent world, that between the efficiency of the free flow of goods and services across national boundaries and the inescapable vulnerability to disruption deriving from that flow. The benefits of an open free-market system and the costs of proliferating deadly transfers clearly grate on one another. It is indeed interesting to note that all six of the ominous transnational flows discussed in this study occur to some degree because of the emergence of an international system norm that the world is a better place if anything and everything can flow freely across national boundaries. While free-market advocates might object that this principle was not meant to include inherently harmful flows, perpetrators of the deadly transfers argue that their activity "is like any other business, with no special moral responsibility."[256] Put simply, the economic "invisible hand" may not function properly in security affairs.

Great difficulty exists in distinguishing clearly acceptable from unacceptable commodities in global exchange (the pervasive nonjudgmental stand mentioned earlier tends to see everything exchanged among nations as "neutral commodities"): differentiating defensive firearms from assault weapons, legal refugees from illegal migrants, over-the-counter stimulants such as alcohol, tobacco, and coffee from illicit drugs, "safe" substances from hazardous materials, mild sicknesses from lethal diseases, and free transmission of ideas from information disruptions involves considerable ambiguity in the eyes of governments and their citizenry and the international community as a whole. This ambiguity, which expands when these distinctions are considered in a cross-cultural context, directly leads to paralysis in action addressing the deadly transfers. Once the unruly members of the global playground sense these differences of interpretation among the monitors, they exploit them to the fullest.

Finally, the reality that these flows generally occur covertly creates what seems to be a nearly insuperable stumbling block for national governments: if they construct more regulations outlawing the transmission of undesired people, technologies, and substances across boundaries, they run the risk of pushing more of this activity underground, making it even harder to detect, more likely in many ways to have dire effects, and easier for the criminal element to dominate cross-national distribution. The choice of doing nothing or watching criminal members of the playground increase their domination seems clearly unacceptable to the world's governments and international organizations. When dealing with transactions that so clearly can fall under the control of the black (or gray) market, traditional legal responses appear to need to be supplanted by different kinds of approaches.

CHANGING INCENTIVES AND ATTITUDES

While this chapter has argued that a deterrence-oriented empowerment of the monitors of the deadly transfers is grossly inadequate to solve the deadly transfer problem, it is equally clear that numerous obstacles have prevented effective forward movement in other directions. To escape from this seeming impasse, this study tentatively suggests a much more challenging strategy—actually changing the incentives facing many players on the global playground so that they no longer see as much utility in engaging in the deadly transfers. It is crucial to note at the outset that this is not to suggest an idealistic solution in which somehow all criminal or terrorist impulses vanish from the planet, but rather a realistic attempt to address the increasing willingness of those normally classified as being well within civil society from indulging in these ominous transnational flows. In other words, if you have a situation where most everyone on the playground sees advantage in misbehaving, restoring order will be well nigh impossible and indeed misbehavior may become the norm; but if the situation is transformed such that only a minority of the players consistently want to misbehave, and the others see much more advantage in conforming to established rules, then not only is it easier to restore order but also those engaging in the misbehavior feel much more negatively sanctioned by the rest of the players.

Part of the trick here is to get the players on the global playground to realize their tight interdependence and the ripple effects of engaging in unsanctioned transactions on the rest of the community. Rather than working to subordinate self-interest to the interests of the community, which would be a real uphill battle given modern individualistic values, there needs to be an effort to show people that it is in their own narrow self-interest to care about broad community concerns when thinking about the deadly transfers. Indeed, at the core here is to increase dramatically the visibility of these negative spillover effects emanating from engaging in immediate, impulsive, self-gratifying behavior that relates to the ominous flows. For this to work the sense of being alienated from an unresponsive community must diminish and be replaced by a system with higher quality communication and greater ability to adapt to changing needs. If all the players who indulge in the flows became more aware not only of the broad negative effects of their behavior on society but also of the personal negative impact of the playground atmosphere on their own ability to enjoy securely the fruits of their participation in the deadly transfers, then their unlawful activities seem more likely to diminish. One crucial prerequisite for this expansion of self-interest to develop properly is that there needs to be time for people to learn more about the collective impact of their individual choices; thus if this awareness is approached in a pressurized crisis atmosphere, true changes in public understanding and attitudes seem remote.

Given the nature of the roadblocks to change, it appears from the preceding analysis that any solution should contain five components. Each attempts to reduce the instigation to engage in deadly transfers on the global playground, rather than simply increasing the inhibitions preventing the outbreak of such activity. These elements place a more direct emphasis on changing individual attitudes rather than on system structure (or on state behavior) because of the grassroots origins of the deadly transfers; the truly transnational nature of this activity does not only involve governments as the primary participants and so should not require governments to be the only primary providers of solutions. The five policy suggestions are (1) confronting those demanding the contraband rather than just those supplying it; (2) perceptually exposing, humiliating, and isolating those engaging in the ominous transnational flows rather than allowing them to continue with both anonymity and respectability; (3) promoting integrated management of all of the ominous flows and of all the players involved in initiating these flows, as opposed to isolated treatment of each; (4) initiating public discussion within governments and between governments and their citizenry about the nature of the tradeoffs involved in the causes and consequences of the deadly transfers, instead of permitting continued avoidance of frank discourse; and (5) fostering a willingness to sacrifice to reduce these transactions and to restore order to the global playground, in place of a rigid insistence that someone or something else must change to solve the problem.

Despite the obvious generality of these ideas, it is possible to see how these suggested components of this strategy to change the prevailing incentive structure on the global playground might work in practice. The focus on addressing demand rather than supply reflects directly the need for attitude change: if people stopped asking for guns, drugs, illegal passports, and the like, then who would the groups attempting to disperse these dangerous commodities sell them to? It seems far too fatalistic to say, as some cynical analysts do, that most people will always desire items like this and that there is nothing one can do about it. A fundamental assumption here is that at least one significant element in recipients' desires for deadly transfers is an ignorance or obliviousness to global negative consequences. A second key premise here is that while curtailing visible supply in the face of continuing demand would simply cause the supply to go underground, curtailing demand in the face of continuing supply would actually reduce the ominous transnational flows themselves. To be fair, though, it is important to note that it is generally a lot more difficult to reduce demand than it is to interdict supply.

At first glance, it would appear that increasing the exposure of those involved in the deadly transfers, with the hope that embarrassment or humiliation would isolate them perceptually so that the rest of the population would see them as aberrant extremists, is an unrealistic dream not reflecting an understanding of the desensitization of the mass public or truly hardened nature of the participants in this activity. After all, have not the disruptive activities of bullies or ruffians on school or park playgrounds occurred with such frequency that those who frequent these places are barely ruffled by them any more? Is it really possible to humiliate these hardened unruly perpetrators? However, this skeptical logic appears to ignore two crucial dimensions of the current predicament. First, many of the initiators and recipients of these ominous transnational flows view themselves (and are viewed by others around them) as upstanding members of their local and national communities, and so image concerns are relevant to them because their success in part depends on interdependent relationships with legitimate enterprises whose respect and trust they need. Second, exposing their involvement in the deadly transfers and tightly linking it with corruption or crime has at least a strong potential to sharpen the set of norms of behavior for the rest of the global community and increase its unity in opposing and marginalizing the guilty parties. National governments, which frequently have considerable complicity in either participating in or turning a blind eye toward the deadly transfers, would appear to be particularly vulnerable to internal and external exposure.[257] Obviously, any emphasis on exposure would need to involve the previously-discussed refocused intelligence activity on the local and global levels to be able to identify definitively those directly involved in these dangerous transactions.

The logic behind the suggestion for integrated management of the six ominous transnational flows and of the players who initiate them is reasonably self-evident given how tightly they are intertwined. If policy makers were to address each set of dangerous transactions in isolation or even sequentially, then as one type of deadly transfer decreased others would appear to have a great likelihood of increasing proportionately. This claim does not assume any kind of implicit, fixed hydraulic model of the ominous transnational flows, in which a downturn in one automatically leads to an upsurge in others; rather it concentrates on the tendencies of certain players (such as transnational criminal organizations) to be involved in several of the flows at once and to develop over time a reliance on certain kinds of expected benefits (in the case of criminal organizations, projected profits), so that when for whatever reason these benefits decrease there would be a natural inclination to try to compensate for this loss through other flows. A similar logic shows why an isolated or sequential focus on each type of perpetrator by policy makers would appear foolhardy: given the tight (though often hidden) links among rogue states, terrorist groups, criminal organizations, and deviant individuals, it would seem that concentrating restraining efforts on one of these without simultaneously addressing the others would simply move existing deadly transfers into a different set of dangerous hands.

Moreover, having not only government security policy makers but also the mass public become more aware of the integrated links among the deadly transfers and among the unruly perpetrators of these flows seems important. This awareness has the potential to diminish both the general willingness to become involved in these flows and the general tolerance of flows initiated by others: for example, both people who use illicit drugs or receive contraband arms and uninvolved people who are aware of these activities may view them as perfectly harmless transfers; but once both groups more fully realize who receives the profits from these activities, where those profits are transferred, how the profits are utilized, and what the broad dangers are, they might be more reluctant to engage in these transactions in the first place or to condone or ignore those who do so. In sum, for both policy makers and the mass public, looking at the big picture helps to increase the likelihood that individual, isolated cross-national transactions that appear relatively innocuous will be linked up to broader global patterns that look a whole lot more ominous.

The issue of public discussion of the predicament of spreading deadly transfers on the global playground is a thinly veiled method for increasing greater public consensus on the issue. Unlike many external security threats completely divorced from the daily activities of a nation's citizenry, these ominous transnational flows directly intrude upon their daily existence. The demand of these citizens for the flows, and their tolerance of the flows, plays an absolutely vital role in the continuation and proliferation of these transactions. Furthermore, such discussion can help those within the mass public who are already aware of the dangers from these flows and consequently opposed to them gain a better understanding of the opportunities and limitations for government action to combat the threats involved. For those members of the public who have responded to the dangers through a fortress mentality bent on securing their own individual safety above all else, open public discussion can highlight the ultimate folly for the community as a whole if this response became widespread. Finally, for government foreign policy officials who feel somewhat paralyzed to deal with such a significant threat emanating from abroad because of its close links to factions within their own society, such discussion could be a vehicle for facilitating greater understanding of how the public can help out and for surfacing new policy options involving joint efforts between the government and the citizenry. Certainly such public discussion has clear limitations, including the inability of such a "town hall" approach to address and resolve highly technical issues (such as those involved in information disruptions) and the possibility that such grassroots dialogue might inadvertently trigger widespread hysteria about the deadly transfers; but it is equally clear that with an ignorant and sharply divided public there can be no effective remedial action.

Mentioning how important it is to foster a widespread willingness to sacrifice among members of the global community may seem laughable to many who see selfish individualism as deeply embedded in modern society and very much at the root of many of the problems discussed in this book. However, it seems reasonably clear that most individuals, groups, and nations continue to feel, even after exposure to the pervasive dangers of the deadly transfers, that their attitudes and behavior can remain unchanged while someone else finds a way to clean up the mess. As long as the attitude persists that these flows and the degenerated state of the playground are someone else's problem and responsibility, forward progress will be stymied. It is important to remember that within each of the six sets of dangerous transactions, the situation is not just that outside groups are wreaking havoc with a nation's

Figure 4
Managing the Global Playground

TRADITIONAL ATTEMPTS TO INCREASE INHIBITIONS

Government-Initiated Changes in System Structure and Security Policy
Applying overwhelming coercive force
Developing restraining international law
Pushing for the legalization of the deadly transfers
Convening international conferences and national government agencies
Reducing the supply of dangerous substances and technologies

UNORTHODOX ATTEMPTS TO DECREASE INSTIGATIONS

Societally-Initiated Changes in Individual Attitudes and Incentives
Promoting public discussion of tradeoffs embedded in deadly transfers
Targeting reduced public demand for deadly transfers
Exposing and humiliating the participants in the deadly transfers
Integrating management of all types of flows and perpetrators
Fostering of a willingness to sacrifice among the mass public

---

citizenry but also that the citizenry is wreaking havoc on itself. Once the responsibility is recognized and accepted, the need for sacrifice seems inescapably to follow. As Senator John Kerry remarks, "the nations of the earth that stand for the rule of civilized law must be willing to make sacrifices if that rule is to endure."[258]

Figure 4 highlights the stark contrast between the instigation-reducing remedies oriented toward changes in individual attitudes advocated by this study and the traditional inhibition-increasing solutions oriented toward government-initiated changes in system structure (and foreign policy-making behavior) frequently advocated elsewhere (discussed earlier in Chapter 3). Of course, efforts in both directions appear necessary to have a truly functional set of policies addressing the deadly transfers, as this study's primary thrust is simply to augment existing strategies—which by themselves have proven to be relatively futile—with an additional set of ideas that appears to operate at a more basic level. Thus to be fair it seems important to realize that both kinds of prescriptions contain inherent weaknesses and dangers in addressing deadly transfers on the global playground.

The traditional structural/behavioral inhibitions include the use of overwhelming coercive force, which seems ineffective due to the failure of deterrence in the post–Cold War setting to manage this kind of threat; the development of restraining international law, which has the potential to push these transactions underground rather than to stop them; the legalization of the deadly transfers, which appears likely to increase their proliferation and penetration into day-to-day activities; the establishment of international conferences and national government agencies focusing on these ominous flows, which appear largely to create a cosmetic "feel-good" reaction that the problem is solved without much tangible progress; and the reduction in the supply of dangerous substances and technologies, which seems to be continually thwarted by a consistent and even growing demand for these contraband items and an open international system that pretty much guarantees that any existing material desires will be satisfied assuming potential buyers can pay the cost. Looking at the overall picture, it does not appear that these structural inhibitions have made much of a dent in the international spread of the deadly transfers, for the increasingly clever perpetrators of these transactions can always seem to find ways to circumvent and thwart the intent of these restraints. While these structural inhibitions try hard to crystallize the international rules of the game for all to see and obey, they fail because the context of this attempt at clarification is an anarchic value system.

Turning to the figure's depiction of remedies oriented toward reducing the attitudinal instigation by individuals to engage in the deadly transfers, there are still numerous pitfalls to overcome despite this study's advocacy of this approach. These transforming attitudinal instigations include the promotion of public discussion of the tradeoffs embedded in the ominous flows, which has the potential to unleash considerable divisiveness and tension among the mass public and between citizens and their governments; the targeting of reduced public demand for these dangerous transactions, which could easily trigger mass public resistance on the grounds that such efforts infringe upon basic civil liberties; the exposure and humiliation of the players involved in the deadly transfers, which could lead to a numb, desensitized, uncaring response rather than the desired marginalization of extremist elements within society; the integrated management of all six types of flows and all four types of perpetrators, which could end up inadvertently stymieing progress in any one direction, as the intertwined nature of the dangerous transactions leaves both policy makers and citizens scratching their heads about where and how to begin; and the fostering of a willingness to sacrifice, which could lead to a major public backlash as people interpret the call for sacrifice as a feeble excuse for government ineffectiveness. The severity of the pitfalls identified here should not be understated.

Despite these challenges, however, it does seem that reducing the attitudinal instigation among individuals to participate in deadly transfers is worth trying (as a way of significantly augmenting the increased behavioral inhibitions), because the mass public is both more intimately involved in these transactions than are governments (which, when not directly involved in these flows, have often turned a blind eye toward them) and potentially more malleable and open to change on this issue due to their incomplete awareness of the scope and depth of the dangers involved. If somehow public tolerance and even encouragement of the deadly transfers were to contract, and the incentive system affecting those engaging in these transactions could change in a manner such that their want or need to do so were to decrease, then there would appear to be a more effective restraining impact on the ominous transnational flows than any effort that leaves the attitudes of participants wanting to engage in these transfers untouched.

CONCLUSION

Many other writings addressing this general area of concern have concluded with an impassioned plea for immediate passage of stricter national policies and strengthened global prohibition regimes to control these ominous transnational flows. In contrast, this analysis has attempted to indicate that neither national governments nor international organizations are yet in any real position to take meaningful behavioral steps in that direction: national hypocrisy and inchoate global rules of the game, buttressed by significant value clashes, a definitional morass about what is acceptable, and a regulatory system seemingly unable to address effectively covert transnational activity, serve to all but stop any forward movement in its tracks. This near-paralysis faced by individual nation-states and the system as a whole reflects a crucial security gap, one not readily remedied by the immediate enactment of new restraining laws, the creation of new bureaucratic agencies, or the escalation of new coercive deterrents. While there is little doubt that an urgent need exists to confront and reduce these flows, it would appear that combined with a macro-focus on improved government action there is great utility in a micro-focus on altered individual attitudes, more fundamentally addressing the reasons they want to engage in these activities.

The kind of solution proposed here has the added benefit of more directly involving the public in taking responsibility for re-solving its own problems instead of pointing its finger at governments and expecting the answers to come from elsewhere. Rather than seeing a dilemma about which they feel they have little un-derstanding and over which they feel they have little control, and thus responding to it in a cowardly or atomistic way reflected by the spread of the individual survivalist mentality and the group move toward gated communities, the approach advocated here appears to have a potential—when combined with more tradi-tional approaches—to stimulate coordinated, collective changes that recognize the direct link between one's own safety and the safety of others. Given the porousness of the international system and the inability of governments to manage effectively on their own many of the kinds of transnational and subnational security threats emerging today, national leaders are likely to welcome this increase in bottom-up assistance in managing the elusive deadly transfers.

Ideally such an approach could lead to a new kind of public-private "burden-sharing" that could be used as a model for ad-dressing other kinds of security concerns as well. If in the process of jointly addressing the ominous transnational flows some com-mon understandings developed about the scope and priority of the mutual dangers involved and about the pervasive dysfunc-tional deficiencies linked to national hypocrisy and crippled global rules of the game evident in responses to these dangers, then there would be a solid foundation for coherent, concerted action that might cause the parties at both the demand end and the supply end of these transactions—those who initiate them, those who facilitate them, and those who receive them—really to take notice. If there is any hope at all in restoring order to the chaotic global playground, it is through this kind of partnership. While there will always be some ruffians and bullies who persist, their behavior can begin to be contained and a common set of rules can become more commonly known and accepted without an intimidating proliferation of restraining monitors. Without a new approach like this one, we can only look forward to seeing the global playground become so rowdy and unprincipled that it ultimately destroys itself.

Notes

1. John P. Sopko, "The Changing Proliferation Threat," *Foreign Policy*, no. 105 (Winter 1996/1997): 7–8.

2. Scott B. MacDonald, "The New 'Bad Guys': Exploring the Parameters of the Violent New World Order," in Max G. Manwaring, ed., *Gray Area Phenomena: Confronting the New World Disorder* (Boulder, CO: Westview Press, 1993), pp. 52–53.

3. Walter Laqueur, "Postmodern Terrorism," *Foreign Affairs*, 75 (September/October 1996): 28; and Sopko, "The Changing Proliferation Threat," pp. 5–6.

4. Louise L. Shelley, "Transnational Organized Crime: An Imminent Threat to the Nation-State?" *Journal of International Affairs*, 48 (Winter 1995): 488–489.

5. Laqueur, "Postmodern Terrorism," p. 34.

6. Phil Williams, "Transnational Criminal Organizations and International Security," *Survival*, 36 (Spring 1994): 109.

7. Senator John Kerry, *The New War* (New York: Simon & Schuster, 1997), p. 26.

8. Brett D. Schaefer, "The International Criminal Court: Threatening U.S. Sovereignty and Security," *Heritage Foundation Executive Memorandum*, no. 537 (July 2, 1998): 1.

9. Roy Godson and Phil Williams, "Strengthening Cooperation Against Transnational Crime," *Survival*, 40 (Autumn 1998): 66.

10. This chapter draws heavily from Robert Mandel, "Deadly Transfers, National Hypocrisy, and Global Chaos," *Armed Forces & Society*, 25 (Winter 1999): forthcoming.

11. Robert Mandel, *The Changing Face of National Security: A Conceptual Analysis* (Westport, CT: Greenwood Press, 1994).

12. Robert Mandel, "What Are We Protecting?" *Armed Forces & Society*, 22 (Spring 1996): 335–355.

13. Matthew Connelly and Paul Kennedy, "Must It Be the Rest Against the West?" *Atlantic Monthly*, 274 (December 1994): 61–91.

14. Scott B. MacDonald, *Dancing on a Volcano: The Latin American Drug Trade* (Westport, CT: Praeger Publishers, 1988), p. 5.

15. Astri Suhrke, "Environmental Degradation and Population Flows," *Journal of International Affairs*, 47 (Winter 1994): 473–496.

16. Martin C. Libicki, "Information War, Information Peace," *Journal of International Affairs*, 51 (Spring 1998): 416–420.

17. Xavier Raufer, "Gray Areas: A New Security Threat," *Political Warfare* (Spring 1992): 2.

18. "Drug Smuggling: Stairway to Heaven," *Economist*, 328 (August 7, 1993): 29.

19. Johan Galtung, *Environment, Development and Military Activity* (Oslo: Universitetsforlaget, 1982), pp. 34–41.

20. This chapter draws heavily from Mandel, "Deadly Transfers, National Hypocrisy, and Global Chaos."

21. Shelley, "Transnational Organized Crime," p. 465.

22. MacDonald, "The New 'Bad Guys,' " pp. 41–42.

23. Joseph S. Nye, Jr., *Understanding International Conflicts* (New York: HarperCollins, 1993), pp. 191–192.

24. Ibid., p. 466.

25. Kerry, *The New War*, p. 20.

26. Ethan A. Nadelmann, "Global Prohibition Regimes: The Evolution of Norms in International Society," *International Organization*, 44 (Autumn 1990): 512.

27. William McNeill, "Winds of Change," in Nicholas X. Rizopoulos, ed., *Sea-Changes* (New York: Council on Foreign Relations Press, 1990), p. 176.

28. Lester Brown, Michael Renner, and Christopher Flavin, *Vital Signs 1998* (New York: W. W. Norton, 1998), p. 161.

29. Lawrence Freedman, "Order and Disorder in the New World," *Foreign Affairs*, 71 (1991/1992): 30.

30. Shelley, "Transnational Organized Crime," p. 468.

31. Brian L. Job, ed., *The Insecurity Dilemma: National Security of Third World States* (Boulder, CO: Lynne Rienner, 1992).

32. Mandel, *The Changing Face of National Security*, pp. 34–35.

33. This chapter draws heavily from Mandel, "Deadly Transfers, National Hypocrisy, and Global Chaos."

34. Lester R. Brown et al., *State of the World 1998* (New York: W. W. Norton, 1998), p. 131.

35. Michael T. Klare, "Secret Operatives, Clandestine Trades: The Thriving Black Market for Weapons," *Bulletin of the Atomic Scientists*, 44 (April 1988): 18–20.

36. Brown et al., *State of the World 1998*, p. 140.

37. "The Covert Arms Trade: The Second-Oldest Profession," *Economist*, 330 (February 12, 1994): 21.

38. Ibid.

39. Brown et al., *State of the World 1998*, p. 133.

40. Raymond Bonner, "21 Nations Seek to Limit Traffic in Light Weapons," *New York Times* (July 13, 1998): A3.

41. R. T. Naylor, "The Structure and Operation of the Modern Arms Black Market," in Jeffrey Boutwell, Michael T. Klare, and Laura W. Reed, eds., *Lethal Commerce* (Cambridge, MA: American Academy of Arts and Sciences, 1995), pp. 45–46.

42. Ibid.

43. Ibid., pp. 48–49.

44. Edward J. Laurance, "The New Gunrunning," *Orbis*, 33 (Spring 1989): 229–232.

45. Edward J. Laurance, "Political Implications of Illegal Arms Exports from the United States," *Political Science Quarterly*, 107 (Fall 1992): 525.

46. Robert Mandel, "Exploding Myths About Global Arms Transfers," *Journal of Conflict Studies*, 18 (Fall 1998): forthcoming.

47. Laurance, "Political Implications of Illegal Arms Exports," p. 525.

48. Brown et al., *State of the World 1998*, p. 131.

49. Ibid., p. 132.

50. Charles M. Sennett, "Armed for Profit: The Selling of US Weapons," *Boston Globe* (February 11, 1996): B2.

51. Keith Krause, *Arms and the State: Patterns of Military Production and Trade* (New York: Cambridge University Press, 1992), p. 195.

52. Frederic S. Pearson, *The Global Spread of Arms* (Boulder, CO: Westview Press, 1994), p. 106.

53. Krause, *Arms and the State*, pp. 196–197.

54. "The Covert Arms Trade," p. 23.

55. Laurance, "The New Gunrunning," p. 225.

56. "The Covert Arms Trade," p. 23.

57. Klare, "Secret Operatives," pp. 16–17; and John Pilger, "Dirty Secrets in Burma," *New Statesman & Society*, 9 (May 10, 1996): 28.

58. "Arming the IRA: The Libyan Connection," *Economist*, 314 (March 31, 1990): 19; and "The Covert Arms Trade," p. 21.

59. Brown et al., *State of the World 1998*, p. 131.

60. Bonner, "21 Nations Seek to Limit Traffic in Light Weapons," p. A3.

61. Gerald L. Sorokin, "Arms, Alliances, and Security Tradeoffs in Enduring Rivalries," *International Studies Quarterly*, 38 (September 1994): 192.

62. Mandel, "Exploding Myths About Global Arms Transfers."

63. Pearson, *The Global Spread of Arms*, pp. 60–61.

64. "The Covert Arms Trade," p. 21; and Aaron Karp, "The Rise of Black and Gray Markets," *Annals of the American Academy of Political and Social Science*, 535 (September 1994): 183–84.

65. "The Covert Arms Trade," pp. 22–23.

66. Mandel, "Exploding Myths About Global Arms Transfers."

67. Karp, "The Rise of Black and Gray Markets," p. 186.

68. Laurance, "Political Implications," p. 506.

69. Laurance, "The New Gunrunning," pp. 232–235.

70. Naylor, "The Structure and Operation of the Modern Arms Black Market," pp. 52–53.

71. This chapter draws heavily from Mandel, "Deadly Transfers, National Hypocrisy, and Global Chaos."

72. "Smuggling Chinese: Heroin Substitute," *Economist*, 327 (May 22, 1993): 33; and "The New Trade in Humans," *Economist*, 336 (August 5, 1995): 45–46.

73. Kerry, *The New War*, pp. 135–36.

74. Demetrios G. Papademetriou, "Migration," *Foreign Policy*, no. 109 (Winter 1997): 22.

75. Kerry, *The New War*, p. 136.

76. Michael Renner, *Fighting for Survival* (New York: W. W. Norton, 1996), pp. 103–104.

77. Papademetriou, "Migration," p. 22.

78. Phyllis Oakley, "Refugee and Migration Crises in a Changing World," Remarks of the Assistant Secretary, Bureau of Population, Refugees, and Migration, U.S. Department of State, to the World Forum of Silicon Valley (San Jose, CA, February 22, 1995), p. 1.

79. Nadelmann, "Global Prohibition Regimes," p. 491.

80. Myron Weiner, *The Global Migration Crisis* (New York: HarperCollins, 1995), pp. 7–8.

81. Ibid., p. 8.

82. Ibid., pp. 5, 8.

83. Jon Vagy, "Sometimes a Crime: Illegal Immigration and Hong Kong," *Crime and Delinquency,* 39 (July 1993): 370.

84. Douglas S. Massey and Kristin E. Espinosa, "What Is Driving Mexico-U.S. Migration? A Theoretical, Empirical, and Policy Analysis," *American Journal of Sociology,* 102 (January 1997): 989–990.

85. "Smuggling Chinese," p. 33; and Kerry, *The New War,* pp. 136–138.

86. Kerry, *The New War,* pp. 143–144.

87. Shada Islam and Adam Schwarz, "Double Deal: Pact on Illegal Migrants Paves Way for EU-Hanoi Talks," *Far Eastern Economic Review,* 158 (February 9, 1995): 28.

88. Kiriro Morita and Suskia Sassen, "The New Illegal Migration in Japan, 1980–1992," *International Migration Review,* 28 (Spring 1994): 153–162.

89. Suhaini Aznam, "Sabah Cuckoo's Nest: Uncontrolled Migration May Tip Political Balance," *Far Eastern Economic Review,* 143 (March 16, 1989): 24–26.

90. James Wiley, "Undocumented Aliens and Recognized Refugees: The Right to Work in Costa Rica," *International Migration Review,* 29 (Summer 1995): 436–437.

91. David Henderson, "International Migration: Appraising Current Policies," *International Affairs,* 70 (1994): 93–110.

92. Robert Mandel, "Perceived Security Threat and the Global Refugee Crisis," *Armed Forces & Society,* 24 (Fall 1997): 77–78.

93. Ibid., pp. 83–85.

94. Kerry, *The New War,* p. 148.

95. Weiner, *The Global Migration Crisis,* p. 3.

96. Ibid., p. 135.

97. Connelly and Kennedy, "Must It Be the Rest Against the West?" p. 69.

98. Weiner, *The Global Migration Crisis,* p. 3.

99. This chapter draws heavily from Mandel, "Deadly Transfers, National Hypocrisy, and Global Chaos."

100. Kerry, *The New War,* p. 87.

101. Louise I. Shelley, "Crime and Corruption in the Digital Age," *Journal of International Affairs,* 51 (Spring 1998): 608.

102. Joseph J. Romm, *Defining National Security: The Nonmilitary Aspects* (New York: Council on Foreign Relations Press, 1993), p. 9.

103. "Poison Across the Rio Grande," *Economist,* 345 (November 15, 1997): 36.

104. Michael Kidron and Ronald Segal, *The State of the World Atlas: New Edition* (New York: Penguin Books, 1995), pp. 72–73.

105. MacDonald, "The New 'Bad Guys,'" p. 37.

106. Kidron and Segal, *The State of the World Atlas,* pp. 72–73.

107. Ibid., p. 144.

108. MacDonald, "The New 'Bad Guys,'" pp. 37–38.

109. Renner, *Fighting for Survival*, p. 192.

110. "Colombia's Drug Business: The Wages of Prohibition," *Economist*, 333 (December 24, 1994): 22.

111. Kerry, *The New War*, p. 88.

112. MacDonald, *Dancing on a Volcano*, pp. 7–8.

113. Nadelmann, "Global Prohibition Regimes," pp. 502–503.

114. Kerry, *The New War*, p. 106.

115. Romm, *Defining National Security*, pp. 9–10.

116. "Colombia's Drug Business," p. 21.

117. MacDonald, *Dancing on a Volcano*, p. 27.

118. Ibid., pp. 28–29.

119. Ibid., pp. 124–134.

120. Kerry, *The New War*, p. 79.

121. Claire Sterling, *Thieves' World* (New York: Simon & Schuster, 1994), p. 21.

122. William O. Walker III, "Drug Trafficking in Asia," *Journal of Interamerican Studies and World Affairs*, 34 (Fall 1992): 210; and Hamish McDonald, "Hooked on Smuggling," *Far Eastern Economic Review*, 157 (June 9, 1994): 34.

123. Romm, *Defining National Security*, p. 9.

124. Rafael F. Perl, "United States Andean Drug Policy: Background and Issues for Decisionmakers," *Journal of Interamerican Studies and World Affairs*, 34 (Fall 1992): 29.

125. Kerry, *The New War*, pp. 82–83.

126. Ibid., pp. 84–86.

127. Kidron and Segal, *The State of the World Atlas*, pp. 72–73.

128. Ibid., p. 144.

129. Ibid.

130. Theodore H. Moran, "International Economics and National Security," *Foreign Affairs*, 69 (Winter 1990/1991): 88–89.

131. Romm, *Defining National Security*, p. 13.

132. MacDonald, *Dancing on a Volcano*, pp. 7–8.

133. "Poison Across the Rio Grande," p. 36.

134. Thomas Land, "Middle East Drug Traffic Set to Rise," *Middle East*, no. 258 (July–August 1996): 20–22.

135. This chapter draws heavily from Mandel, "Deadly Transfers, National Hypocrisy, and Global Chaos."

136. Jang B. Singh and V. C. Lakhan, "Business Ethics and the International Trade in Hazardous Wastes," *Journal of Business Ethics*, 8 (November 1989): 889–890.

137. Sean D. Murphy, "Prospective Liability Regimes and the Trans-

boundary Movement of Hazardous Wastes," *American Journal of International Law,* 88 (January 1994): 25, 29.

138. Singh and Lakhan, "Business Ethics," pp. 889–890; and Brian R. Copeland, "International Trade in Waste Products in the Presence of Illegal Disposal," *Journal of Environmental Economics and Management,* 20 (March 1991): 143.

139. Murphy, "Prospective Liability Regimes," p. 30.

140. "Let Them Eat Pollution," *Economist,* 322 (February 8, 1992): 66; "Pollution and the Poor," *Economist,* 322 (February 15, 1992): 18–19; and Singh and Lakhan, "Business Ethics," p. 890.

141. Copeland, "International Trade," p. 48.

142. Murphy, "Prospective Liability Regimes," p. 31; and "Uranium, Plutonium, Pandemonium," *Economist,* 327 (June 5, 1993): 98.

143. Murphy, "Prospective Liability Regimes," p. 25; and Singh and Lakhan, "Business Ethics," p. 889.

144. Singh and Lakhan, "Business Ethics," pp. 889, 895.

145. Robin Ajello and Arjuna Ranawana, "The West's Toxic Trade with Asia," *World Press Review,* 43 (December 1996): 31.

146. Kerry, *The New War,* p. 116; Graham T. Allison, Owen R. Cote, Jr., Richard A. Falkenrath, and Steven E. Miller, *Avoiding Nuclear Anarchy* (Cambridge, MA: MIT Press, 1996), p. 7; and "The Plutonium Racket," *Economist,* 332 (August 20, 1994): 39–40.

147. Sopko, "The Changing Proliferation Threat," p. 10.

148. Murphy, "Prospective Liability Regimes," p. 67.

149. "Toxic Shock," *New Statesman & Society,* 2 (August 18, 1989): 11.

150. Ajello and Ranawana, "The West's Toxic Trade with Asia," p. 31.

151. Singh and Lakhan, "Business Ethics," pp. 893, 896.

152. "Muck and Morals," *Economist,* 336 (September 2, 1995): 61.

153. Ann Leonard and Jan Rispens, "Exposing the Recycling Hoax: Bharat Zinc and the Politics of the International Waste Trade," *Multinational Monitor,* 17 (January–February 1996): 30.

154. Ibid.

155. Ibid., pp. 30–34.

156. Ajello and Ranawana, "The West's Toxic Trade with Asia," p. 31.

157. Rob Edwards, "Dirty Tricks in a Dirty Business," *New Scientist,* 145 (February 18, 1995): 12.

158. Ibid., pp. 12–13.

159. Ibid.

160. Allison, Cote, Falkenrath, and Miller, *Avoiding Nuclear Anarchy,* p. 11.

161. Kerry, *The New War,* pp. 116–17.

162. Shelley, "Transnational Organized Crime," p. 468.

163. "Uranium, Plutonium, Pandemonium," p. 98.

164. William H. McNeill, *Plagues and Peoples* (New York: Doubleday, 1977), p. 5.

165. "Clinton Girds U.S. for Terrorism War," *USA Today* (May 22, 1998): 1.

166. Laurie Garrett, "The Return of Infectious Disease," *Foreign Affairs*, 75 (January/February 1996): 74, 78.

167. S. Jay Olshansky, Bruce Carnes, Richard G. Rogers, and Len Smith, "Infectious Diseases—New and Ancient Threats to World Health," *Population Bulletin*, 52 (July 1997): 5.

168. Lester R. Brown, Christopher Flavin, and Hal Kane, *Vital Signs 1996* (New York: W. W. Norton, 1996), p. 130.

169. Olshansky et al., "Infectious Diseases," p. 8.

170. Brown, Flavin, and Kane, *Vital Signs 1996*, p. 130.

171. Garrett, "The Return of Infectious Disease," p. 73.

172. Olshansky et al., "Infectious Diseases," pp. 7–8.

173. James H. Anderson, "Microbes and Mass Casualties: Defending America Against Bioterrorism," *Heritage Foundation Backgrounder*, no. 1182 (May 26, 1998): 3.

174. Ibid., p. 1.

175. Ibid., p. 3.

176. Garrett, "The Return of Infectious Disease," p. 66,

177. Ibid., p. 67.

178. Olshansky et al., "Infectious Diseases," pp. 2–3.

179. Ibid., p. 3.

180. Richard K. Betts, "The New Threat of Mass Destruction," *Foreign Affairs*, 77 (January/February 1998): 38.

181. Sopko, "The Changing Proliferation Threat," p. 9.

182. Olshansky et al., "Infectious Diseases," pp. 3–4.

183. Garrett, "The Return of Infectious Disease," p. 72.

184. Ibid.

185. Olshansky et al., "Infectious Diseases," pp. 19–20.

186. Garrett, "The Return of Infectious Disease," pp. 72–73.

187. Anderson, "Microbes and Mass Casualties," pp. 3–5.

188. Dennis Pirages, "Microsecurity: Disease Organisms and Human Well-Being," *Washington Quarterly*, 18 (Autumn 1995): 11.

189. Laqueur, "Postmodern Terrorism," p. 29.

190. Garrett, "The Return of Infectious Disease," p. 70.

191. Ibid., p. 76

192. Anderson, "Microbes and Mass Casualties," pp. 6–8.

193. Ibid., p. 8.

194. Joshua Lederberg, "Infectious Disease and Biological Weapons: Prophylaxis and Mitigation," *Journal of the American Medical Association*, 278 (August 6, 1997): 435–436.

195. Garrett, "The Return of Infectious Disease," p. 69.

196. Brown, Renner, and Flavin, *Vital Signs 1998*, p. 106.

197. Kerry, *The New War*, pp. 127–128.

198. Richard O. Hundley and Robert H. Anderson, "Emerging Challenge: Security and Safety in Cyberspace," in John Arquilla and David Ronfeldt, eds., *In Athena's Camp: Preparing for Conflict in the Information Age* (Santa Monica, CA: RAND Corporation, 1997), p. 231.

199. Libicki, "Information War, Information Peace," p. 417.

200. Chris O'Malley, "Information Warriors of the 609th," *Popular Science*, 251 (July 1997): 70–74.

201. Ibid.

202. John Arquilla and David Ronfeldt, "Cyberwar Is Coming!" in Arquilla and Ronfeldt, eds., *In Athena's Camp*, p. 23.

203. John Arquilla and David Ronfeldt, "Information, Power, and Grand Strategy in Athena's Camp—Section 1," in Arquilla and Ronfeldt, eds., *In Athena's Camp*, p. 141.

204. Jeffrey R. Cooper, *The Emerging Infosphere* (McLean, VA: Center for Information Strategy and Policy at Science Applications International Corporation, August 1997), p. 25.

205. John Arquilla and David Ronfeldt, "A New Epoch—and Spectrum—of Conflict," in Arquilla and Ronfeldt, eds., *In Athena's Camp*, p. 5.

206. Kerry, *The New War*, p. 123.

207. Hundley and Anderson, "Emerging Challenge," p. 232.

208. Kerry, *The New War*, pp. 121, 124, 126, 128.

209. William B. Scott, "Information Warfare Policies Called Critical to National Security," *Aviation Week and Space Technology*, 145 (October 28, 1996): 60.

210. "Clinton Girds U.S. for Terrorism War," p. 1.

211. Bruce D. Berkowitz, "Warfare in the Information Age," *Issues in Science and Technology*, 12 (Fall 1995), pp. 59–66.

212. Libiciki, "Information War, Information Peace," pp. 411–412.

213. Ibid., pp. 416–417.

214. Shelley, "Crime and Corruption in the Digital Age," pp. 605–606.

215. Ibid., pp. 606–611.

216. Berkowitz, "Warfare in the Information Age," pp. 59–66.

217. Laqueur, "Postmodern Terrorism," p. 35.

218. Ibid.

219. Brian Nichiporuk and Carl H. Builder, "Societal Implications," in Arquilla and Ronfeldt, eds., *In Athena's Camp*, pp. 296–297.

220. Shelley, "Crime and Corruption in the Digital Age," pp. 613–615.

221. Ibid., pp. 613–614.

222. This chapter draws heavily from Mandel, "Deadly Transfers, National Hypocrisy, and Global Chaos."

223. Michael T. Klare, *American Arms Supermarket* (Austin: University of Texas Press, 1984), p. 27.

224. "Chinese Yearning to Work Free," *Economist*, 328 (July 24, 1993): 38; "The New Trade in Humans," pp. 45–46; and Vagy, "Sometimes a Crime," p. 372.

225. Romm, *Defining National Security*, p. 9.

226. Perl, "United States Andean Drug Policy," pp. 25–29.

227. "Colombia's Drug Business," p. 22.

228. Luis Suarez Salazar, " 'Drug Trafficking' and Social and Political Conflicts in Latin America," *Latin American Perspectives*, 20 (Winter 1993): 91.

229. Murphy, "Prospective Liability Regimes," p. 32; Singh and Lakhan, "Business Ethics," pp. 897–898; and "Uranium, Plutonium, Pandemonium," pp. 98–100.

230. "Old Horrors," *Economist*, 327 (May 29, 1993): 15–16; and Singh and Lakhan, "Business Ethics," 890.

231. "Deadly Secret," *Economist*, 333 (December 3, 1994): 46.

232. Pirages, "Microsecurity," p. 11.

233. Garrett, "The Return of Infectious Disease," p. 76.

234. Ibid.

235. U.S. Air Force, *Cornerstones of Information Warfare* (Washington, DC: Department of the Air Force, 1995), pp. 3–4.

236. Berkowitz, "Warfare in the Information Age," pp. 59–66.

237. This chapter draws heavily from Mandel, "Deadly Transfers, National Hypocrisy, and Global Chaos."

238. Zeev Maoz, *Paradoxes of War* (Boston: Unwin Hyman, 1990), p. 9. See also Stephen Krasner, ed., *International Regimes* (Ithaca, NY: Cornell University Press, 1983).

239. William J. Olson, "The New World Disorder: Governability and Development," in Manwaring, ed., *Gray Area Phenomena*, p. 9.

240. Max G. Manwaring and Courtney E. Prisk, "The Umbrella of Legitimacy," in Manwaring, ed., *Gray Area Phenomena*, p. 90.

241. Maoz, *Paradoxes of War*, p. 327.

242. Godson and Williams, "Strengthening Cooperation," p. 66.

243. Andrew P. Cortell and James W. Davis, Jr., "How Do International Institutions Matter? The Domestic Impact of International Rules and Norms," *International Studies Quarterly*, 40 (December 1996): 451–478.

244. Kerry, *The New War*, p. 190.

245. Ibid., p. 171.

246. Robert Mandel, "Distortions in the Intelligence Decision-Making Process," in Stephen J. Cimbala, ed., *Intelligence and Intelligence Policy in a Democratic Society* (Dobbs Ferry, NY: Transnational Publishers, 1987), p. 79.

247. James B. Motley, "Coping with the Terrorist Threat: The U.S. Intelligence Dilemma," in Cimbala, ed., *Intelligence and Intelligence Policy*, p. 169.

248. Mandel, "What Are We Protecting?" p. 352.

249. Mandel, "Exploding Myths About Global Arms Transfers."

250. National Strategy Information Center, *The Gray Area Phenomenon* (Washington, DC: National Strategy Information Center, July 1992), p. 8; and Roy Godson and William J. Olson, *International Organized Crime: Emerging Threat to U.S. Security* (Washington, DC: National Strategy Information Center, August 1993), pp. 18–19.

251. Renner, *Fighting for Survival*, p. 22.

252. Brown et al., *State of the World 1998*, pp. 135–136.

253. Mandel, *The Changing Face of National Security*, p. 135.

254. Freedman, "Order and Disorder in the New World," p. 37.

255. William D. Hartung, *And Weapons for All* (New York: Harper-Perennial, 1995), pp. 288–289.

256. Anthony Sampson, *The Arms Bazaar* (New York: Viking Press, 1977), pp. 329, 340.

257. Kerry, *The New War*, p. 183.

258. Ibid., p. 187.

Selected Bibliography

Boutwell, Jeffrey, Klare, Michael T., and Reed, Laura W., eds. *Lethal Commerce*. Cambridge, MA: American Academy of Arts and Sciences, 1995.

Godson, Roy, and Olson, William J. *International Organized Crime: Emerging Threat to U.S. Security*. Washington, DC: National Strategy Information Center, August 1993.

Kerry, Senator John. *The New War*. New York: Simon & Schuster, 1997.

Mandel, Robert. *The Changing Face of National Security: A Conceptual Analysis*. Westport, CT: Greenwood Press, 1994.

Manwaring, Max G., ed. *Gray Area Phenomena: Confronting the New World Disorder*. Boulder, CO: Westview Press, 1993.

McNeill, William. "Winds of Change." In Nicholas X. Rizopoulos, ed., *Sea-Changes*. New York: Council on Foreign Relations Press, 1990, pp. 163–203.

Nadelmann, Ethan A. "Global Prohibition Regimes: The Evolution of Norms in International Society." *International Organization*, 44 (Autumn 1990): 479–526.

Renner, Michael. *Fighting for Survival*. New York: W. W. Norton, 1996.

Romm, Joseph J. *Defining National Security: The Nonmilitary Aspects*. New York: Council on Foreign Relations Press, 1993.

Sterling, Claire. *Thieves' World*. New York: Simon & Schuster, 1994.

Index

About the Author

ROBERT MANDEL is Chair and Professor of International Affairs at Lewis and Clark College in Portland, Oregon. He has written five books and numerous articles and chapters dealing primarily with security and conflict issues. He has testified before the United States Congress and worked for the Central Intelligence Agency, the Defense Department, and the United States Institute of Peace.

ISBN 0-275-96228-8

90000>

EAN

9 780275 962289

HARDCOVER BAR CODE